SHORELANDS SUMMER DIARY

GATEWAY TO ANGLESEY

SHORELANDS
· SUMMER ·
Diary

CLIVE HOLLOWAY BOOKS

LONDON

First published by William Collins Sons & Co. Ltd., in 1952
This edition published in 1984 by
Clive Holloway Books
205 Victoria Rise
London SW4 9LJ

British Library Cataloguing in Publication data

Tunnicliffe, C. F.
    Shorelands summer diary
    1. Bird watching – Wales – Anglesey
    2. Title
    598'.07'23442921   QL690.G7

ISBN 0-907745-03-02

Printed in Italy

CONTENTS

FOREWORD

CHARLES and Winifred Tunnicliffe fell in love with Shorelands the moment they set eyes upon it. When it came up for sale they bought it and moved from Macclesfield to the island of Anglesey in March 1947. They were into middle age and the move heralded the summer time of their lives. Few young couples of their generation could have worked harder, Charles at his easel and Winifred as a teacher and housewife. Their married life up to the spring of 1947 had been spent in surroundings that were far from inspiring, but by the time they moved Charles Tunnicliffe was a full member of the Royal Academy and widely acclaimed for his bird portraiture as well as illustrative art He had always been determined to fulfill himself as an artist who would paint and draw what he felt inspired to do. He was equally determined to escape suburbia and work in a place where his subjects were available on his doorstep. In this both husband and wife were in complete accord. An artist in her own right, Winifred too, had been a graduate of the Royal College of Art, and on Anglesey she found herself almost as much in love with Shorelands as she was with her gifted husband. They had discovered the place together. They settled there with great expectations that were realised. A couple who needed only each other, it might have been said by some people that Winifred was both wife and mother to Charles Tunnicliffe. Certainly she bolstered his confidence and made a wonderful home of Shorelands. The world promised to beat a path to their door, and it did, but Winifred was there, with great understanding and devotion, to see that her hard-working husband in that studio looking out on the estuary wasn't disturbed. Charles could put in his twelve hour day and regularly did so, knowing that everything that might come up was being handled with firmness and tact by Winifred. Publishers called him frequently. The bell rang in that quiet house and Winifred answered it, holding them off when she knew Charles was involved with something more important than a printer's deadline. Fans who knocked at the door might be given tea and scones, departing without seeing the artist except as a figure hunched at the drawing board. Shorelands was, in fact, a kind of Shangri-la for the Tunnicliffes, a place of peace and contentment where the only sound would be the trilling of waders, the yelping of gulls and other seabirds while on the shore a cormorant hung out his wings to dry looking like a Germanic war standard. Alas, time went faster and faster as it does in idyllic surroundings. The diary marked high noon. Summer ended and Winifred died. Neither of them had ever been long away from this place and Charles Tunnicliffe lived on there until, in February 1979, almost blind and no longer able to see to paint, he died, sitting in his chair by the fire. Winter had finally come to Shorelands. The Diary constitutes an impressive momento of the life, the summer time, of an artist whose work delighted and gave great pleasure to thousands of people not only in Britain but throughout the world.

Ian Niall
"Five Acres" 1984

Colour Illustrations

THE WINDING LANE TO THE HOUSE

INTRODUCTION

ON THE evening of March the 27th, my wife and I crossed over Telford's great bridge which spans the Menai Straits, and entered the island county of Anglesey. We were no strangers to this fair country, but our journey to-day was different from all previous ones for, at the end of it, in a little grey village at the head of an estuary, there was an empty house which we hoped to call home as soon as we could get our belongings into it. Our other visits had been short holidays, spent chiefly in watching and drawing birds and landscape of which there was great variety. Several sketch-books had been filled with studies of Anglesey and its birds, and we had been specially delighted to find that the island in spring and autumn was a calling place for many migratory birds, while summer and winter had their own particular and different species. Occasionally, to add to the excitement, a rarity would appear. Whatever the season there were always birds and this fact had greatly influenced us in our choice of a new home.

Our intention to establish ourselves in this Celtic land was not to be accomplished without opposition however, for Anglesey, the Mother of Wales, had built a little church on one side of our lane, and the stone wall of a cottage garden on the other. The furniture vans were monstrous and stuck fast between church and garden wall and could proceed no farther. After we had scratched our heads in perplexity, and listened to suggestions from interested observers, Môn Mam Cymru relented and sent a coal lorry to our aid. The sun shone, the furniture went into the house via the coal lorry, and the Shelducks on the sands laughed and cackled all day.

9

HIGH TIDE OVER THE GARDEN WALL

There followed days of arranging and re-arranging and gradually order emerged from chaos, the proceedings often suspended while we gazed from the windows. Field-glasses and telescope were always kept in readiness for a sudden grab, but it was astonishing how often they became buried under other material not yet put in its proper place. Such was the case when we heard the call of wild geese one evening. Books and paper went flying, field-glasses were unearthed, raised and focussed on a fine skein of Grey Lags as they flew past the house and down the estuary. What a grand clamour they made! We watched them until, with impetuous tumbles, they came to rest on the sands two miles away. Wild geese viewed from our own front door! it was a warming thought, and as we watched there were other small but significant happenings. Stonechats haunted the gorsey patch beyond the lounge window, often perching on the boundary wall and gazing in at us. Yellow-hammers, which were surely more vivid in colour than the Cheshire Yellow-hammers, flitted about this same wild patch, and about the old stone walls Wrens hunted confidingly. We felt that we had made a good choice.

THE S-BEND

BRIDGE, ROAD, FIELD POOLS AND COB LAKE

The house is well named " Shorelands " for only a stout stone wall and a row of rough upright timbers protect it from the tides of a mile-wide estuary. Years ago the estuary extended almost into the very heart of the island, but in the year 1812 a sea wall was built, and the inland area over which the tides used to flood was reclaimed and is now good farmland, dotted about with grey stone farmsteads, and intersected by numerous dykes and raised earth banks. The sea wall is called locally " The Cob," and it has its beginning very close to the village at a spot where a bridge spans the river and its two flood-water canals. River and canals are disciplined by high man-made banks for some miles inland, indeed as far as the river is tidal. The bridge marks the end of the village street and the beginning of the road over the marsh. After crossing the bridge the road swings slightly inland, then deviates shorewards again and touches the Cob at its far end. Thus, between Cob and road, there is an area of brackish pool and swamp which is beloved of the birds, and both road and Cob make ideal vantage points for their study. Many are the happy hours I have spent there. The pool in this diary is called " Cob Lake." On the other side of the road are fields which are often flooded and, even in summer, are rarely without water. Here too the birds love to congregate, and there have been occasions when I have not known which way to turn, Cob Lake or field pools, because of the richness of bird-life on them.

But to return home: the windows in the front of the house command views from east to south-west. Looking south-east, with the Cob extending across its whole width, is the mile-wide estuary. Beyond, filling the middle distance, is a long ridge of high ground crisscrossed by hedges and dotted about with farms, which at its seaward end deteriorates into rock and sand-dune, and above this ridge loom the great mountains of Caernarvonshire, the kingdom of Eryri, with Snowdon lording it over all—a stupendous panorama. The view looking south, if not so high and mighty, is just as good, for now the river, after running

11

parallel with the house, makes a lovely S-bend across the sands before turning again to meander to the sea. Still looking south the ridge of the middle distance is now sand-dune, and just over the curve of a wind-scalloped hollow a little white speck can be discerned—the top of the lighthouse on Llandwyn Island three miles away. Beyond rise the shapely blue hills of Lleyn with the tree peaks which the English call " The Rivals," and whose proper name is Yr Eifl, which means " The Forks," looking much higher than they are in reality, for their steep sides fall sheer to the sea. To the south-west Lleyn continues in a series of lesser hills, losing itself eventually below the sea horizon beyond the bar, and then appearing on the horizon again like an island which is, I suspect, Mynydd Anelog at the very end of Lleyn.

From the house to the bar, the distance is nearly three miles, three miles of sand through which the river winds its serpentine way, sands which hold thousands, nay, tens of thousands, of birds. It may have been these sands which gave our village its name of Malltraeth—which in English means the " Bad Strand," for I have no doubt that to the sailors of old it was a wild and dangerous place in stormy weather.

On March the 29th I took a walk along the Cob and, to my delight and surprise (for I had not previously seen this species in Anglesey), I found two Great-crested Grebes swimming on Cob Lake. It was good to know that in leaving my native Cheshire I had not necessarily cut myself off from these strange and interesting birds, and I wondered if they nested in Anglesey or whether they were just birds of passage. They were slim and alert as they watched my progress along the Cob. With them swam a solitary Pochard drake with a fine copper-red head and neck. Neither he nor his Grebe companions bothered to dive, safe as they were in the middle of the lake. Out on the sands Shelduck fed in groups and often the ducks sent out their weird witch-like calls. How immaculate they were in their spring plumage! The drakes were growing the knob at the base of their bills, that special decoration for the breeding season, indeed in some drakes it appeared well-grown.

THE COB

12

On the far saltings the Curlew were calling and, as I watched, some of them came up the estuary and, flying almost overhead, continued up the marsh, suddenly soaring up and sideways as a shot rang out from a rabbiting farmer.   Away into the distance of the marsh they sped, calling, calling all the way, an exquisite choir.   I returned along the Cob, past the Welsh Black cattle grazing there, and, for a time, watched the homing gulls as they flew in formation down the marsh, over the Cob to their roosting place on the sands.   Then I, too, went homeward, full of hope and anticipation of riches to come.

RED-BREASTED MERGANSER

APRIL

APRIL 1ST. Affairs in the house becoming more settled I spent this morning in the studio, unearthing and arranging books and equipment, my labours often interrupted by the enchantment which lay beyond the studio window. Through the telescope I gazed at Redshanks, Oystercatchers, Shelduck and Gulls which dotted the sands. (It will take some time to get used to the fact that these birds, and many others, are to be seen from my window just for the looking.) Then I had my first thrill for, in the middle of the river, a bird suddenly surfaced and the telescope revealed a Red-breasted Merganser, a fine drake with streaming crest. Almost at once he dived again, surfacing next much farther down the river. He traversed the length of the S-bend in long dives and was lost to sight.

In the late afternoon when the tide had ebbed, leaving bright sky-reflecting sand, I walked along the northern shore of the estuary to where the Bodorgan fields terminate abruptly in low cliffs covered with blackthorn and bramble. Here, in a rocky cranny, I took shelter for the wind was from the north-east and was cold. The mountain tops were streaked and veined with snow, and Snowdon's peak was solidly white. Presently the antics of two Carrion-crows attracted my attention. The crows ascended vertically, the wind lifting them without a wing-beat. At a height of thirty feet they dropped what I believe were mussels on to the sand below, following them quickly and alighting an instant after the mussels had touched ground. These they picked up again in their bills, and again made the same effortless ascent, and again dropped the dark objects on to the soft sand. Many times they repeated this manœuvre, which, if it was an attempt to break the shells, was quite unsuccessful. (I had an idea that crows were too intelligent to make this type of mistake.) Then I think they must have seen a glint from my field-glasses for, with deep " quarks " both birds left hurriedly and, flying into the teeth of the wind, beat away up the marsh.

Where the shore is littered with stones and boulders a Greenshank sheltered, its slim pale form huddled and facing the wind. It granted me only thirty seconds of study and then, it too, was away, uttering a high mournful note.

14

SHELTERING GREENSHANK

APRIL 4TH. A perfect spring day of warm sunlight, and blue sky against which the mountains were clear and distinct. At mid-morning three Lesser Black-backed Gulls appeared in front of the house. They were noisy and, as they flew, postured with bent necks, and continued to do so as they alighted by the river. They are the first I have seen this year and are, no doubt, part of the breeding population of Bodorgan headland. At noon, on Cob Lake, I was watching a party of Redshank feeding in the shallows when I noticed among them a taller, greyer bird which, in its manner of feeding, was more vigorous than the common Redshanks. It had red legs but its plumage was beautifully marked with dusky blotches on neck, breast, and flanks. I had no doubt but that it was a Spotted Redshank, probably a young bird changing from first winter to first summer plumage. Sometimes it was bullied by the Common Redshanks, and once was chased into deep water so that it appeared to be afloat. (On previous visits I have seen Spotted Redshanks but they have always occurred in the autumn, and have, invariably, been young birds.)

Towards evening the light and colour became more intense, revealing in the mountains, precipices, edges, and chasms unsuspected before. A great concourse of Gulls gathered on the sands at the edge of the river and there must have been many thousands of them. They looked like a drift of snow by the river bank.

As the sun sank, and the mountains were taking on a rosy colour, the calling of geese

TWO COMMON AND A SPOTTED REDSHANK

15

GEESE FLYING UP THE MARSH

was heard from the bar, and soon a long, thin, undulating line was seen advancing swiftly up the estuary. Steadily they came on and the line resolved itself into a wavering V-formation of about a hundred and fifty birds. The character of the formation changed constantly, and frequently individuals swung across from one arm of the V to the other. They were Grey Lags and noisy as usual and, as they came opposite the house, the last rays of the setting sun lit up their undersides. Over the Cob and up the marsh they went, calling all the time, the sounds gradually growing fainter until the birds were lost to sight in the distance.

Later, when the moon had risen against a night sky of dappled cloud, we heard geese passing again and, these too, were flying in a north-easterly direction and we wondered if this was farewell until next October.

APRIL 5TH. What a change! Yesterday all smiles, to-day a glowering grey sky and a blustering wind which, at noon, roared up from the south-west bringing with it a tide whose breakers slapped the shore wall to send spray flying over the garden. Then rain came and by mid-afternoon the downpour was thrust almost horizontal by a wind which reached gale force and found all the cracks and crannies in window-frames and all faulty slates. When the storm was at its height there was a crashing rumble on the roof and fragments of rough-casting went flying past the window like bits of paper. When it was fit to go outside we found that the rough-cast face of one of the chimneys had been torn away and the brickwork exposed.

Gulls flew low over the sands and even then had the greatest difficulty in forging ahead. Cormorants were unable to make any progress and often turned and were driven before the gale. The storm abated during the night.

16

APRIL 8TH. To-day flood-water was everywhere. A night of rain and a day of heavy snow-storms (in which the flakes were a fantastic size) characterised the preceding twenty-four hours, and every hollow was now a pool. The garage was unapproachable except when wearing waders, and the white entrance gates were reflected in a large pool which threatened to cut off communication with the village. The river, and its two parallel channels, stretching in magnificent perspective up the marsh, brought their flood waters to the narrow gullet of the road bridge, through which they roared in brown swollen spate to spread across the sands in a river twice its normal width.

The road which descends from the village and skirts Cob Lake was only just above the water-level, and great stretches of the marsh fields on the other side of the road were still lakes reflecting farms, fences and mountains, beautiful to the eye of the artist but a scourge to the marsh farmers. The latest snowstorms had covered the mountains afresh and Snowdon was completely white.

Since the storm of April 5th my two Stonechats have disappeared from the brambles by the garden wall, and the gulls have not once congregated in their usual place on the estuary sand.

APRIL 9TH. Soft air and sunlight enticed us out this afternoon to Porth Cwyfan, a few miles along the coast. Porth Cwyfan is a bay, a rather rough and untidy bay of rocks, sand, and shingle, but a place which never fails to produce birds. It is a place of some curiousness, for jutting up from its waters is a grass-topped islet, fortified all around by courses of masonry, and on its top is a tiny church. On old maps the church is shown as part of the mainland, but years of wild seas have gradually worn away the low cliffs of boulder clay, biting deeper and deeper into the land, until now the little church is many yards from the shore, and is joined to the beach by a causeway of shingle and boulders. To-day Turnstones were hunting the weed by the causeway, burying their heads beneath a clump and throwing it over with the utmost vigour. Stones, quite large stones, were treated in the same manner, and there was intermittent clatter as the birds hunted.

On the green fields skirting the bay gulls bathed in the bright blue pools left by the floods, and close by Welsh sheep and their white, pretty lambs grazed or rested peacefully. (I think the lambs of the Welsh mountain breed are probably the prettiest of all lambs, and they rarely fail to draw choruses of sentimental utterances from the female sex.)

Old stone farms stood on the skyline, sunlit and rugged, and behind it all loomed the stately mountains with their snow mantles gleaming white, and their shadows pale blue. Later,

RIVER AND SIDE-CHANNEL IN FLOOD

17

PORTH CWYFAN

from the studio window, I watched the clouds shadow the mountains until only Snowdon was lit, golden-white against a limpid green-blue sky.

APRIL 13TH. The flood-waters have subsided and the field pools are almost down to their winter level. Friend Wack came down this evening and, as usual, our noses turned automatically towards Cob Lake and the pools. In spite of the cold breeze which rippled the waters the air was full of the trilling of amorous Redshanks, and presently we watched a male move into the first position of the display. He dropped the fore-part of his body in a half-crouch, one wing was lowered below his tail, which was half-opened, depressed and carried slightly to one side, and in this posture he approached a female. When about five feet from her he suddenly opened his wings, raised his head and, almost dancing, vibrated his still open wings displaying the pattern of white to great effect, so that he looked like a large and elegant butterfly. Slowly, seemingly on tiptoe, trilling all the time, he danced towards the female and drew level with her. For the first time she deigned to notice him as he circled round her, his wings still vibrating. Gradually he circled until he was behind her, then his wings seemed to beat even more quickly, his feet left the ground and for a few moments he hovered above her. Suddenly she ran away from him and he dropped to earth folding his butterfly wings to his side. Adopting the first crouching position he again approached her, but she would have none of him, and always ran away just as he commenced to hover. Later we watched another pair and, this time the display was carried to its completion, the male hovering above the female for some moments then, gently lowering himself until his tarsi rested along her back, he dropped his tail to one side of her tail and, with a sudden movement, the mating was completed. She ran from under him, shook her feathers, and became sleek once more, and he, for a few moments, went into the crouched position with tail depressed, then commenced to feed.

So interested had we been in this beautiful display of the Redshanks that it was some time before we noted a bird feeding with them, which was much paler of head and neck. It had

18

greenish legs and its bill was shorter than the Redshank's. The telescope was used and revealed that it was a female Ruff. Delicately it stepped about the mud, pecking here and there, and, as it came closer, we noted the thin dark bars across the neck, marks of summer plumage. Wack and I agreed that anything might happen in this place, and we talked hopefully of Avocets and Spoonbills. A Glossy Ibis occurred on Cob Lake some winters ago.

MALE WING-VIBRATING AND TRILLING

APRIL 15TH. Since yesterday a sea mist has obliterated all distances and visibility has varied from a few hundred yards to a mile. Rarely has the end of the Cob, a mile away, been visible. The mist has persisted in spite of the strong breeze which, one would have thought, would have cleared all mist away.

MALE HOVERING ABOVE FEMALE

All day the ghostly shapes of Shelduck have shown momentarily above the level top of the Cob, as they have flown up in excited chases of rivalry from the lake behind. In the evening I went out to investigate all this excitement, and found sixteen Shelduck on the lake, mostly in pairs, where they were not hopelessly mixed up in squabbles. I watched one drake approach a duck and begin a peculiar and repeated action of the head and neck, a kind of up and down pot-hook action, and while he postured, he whistled continuously, a whistle rather like a muted Redshank trill. His duck answered with a harsh and loud "Gargh! Gargh!" while she lowered her neck and head along the water and swung it from side to side. Presently another drake approached the still posturing pair and, arching his neck attacked the duck by gripping her nape. Her own drake, after recovery from his surprise rushed in, and there was a wild flurry in which it was just possible to see that one drake had the other by the neck. Then one broke away and with a rush took wing, hotly followed by his rival who was almost on his tail when the leading drake zoomed vertically upwards. The sight of both drakes ascending, with wings and tail widespread, was a fine one; it was grand impetuous flying. The chase did not last long, the outraged drake returning to his duck and greeting her with more vigorous bowings and posturing. "Coo! Coo! Coo! Coo!" he

REDSHANKS MATING

19

RUFF

whistled. "Gargh! Gargh! Gargh!" replied she. One drake which had been chased from the lake by a rival came down on Bont Farm pool, gliding sideways in the breeze on arched wings, and ploughing the water in two jets as his spread rosy webs brought him to a standstill. There, in the middle of the rippled expanse, with no other duck in sight, he bowed and bowed. Strange birds!

Out on the estuary sands a flock of between twenty and thirty Shelduck rested amicably together, seemingly untroubled by seasonal urges and rivalries.

SHELDUCKS ON COB LAKE

20

WHITE WAGTAILS

APRIL 16TH. This evening, on the grassy flats between the field pools, two rough-coated shire horses were grazing, and near their hoofs and noses Wagtails hunted the grass, twinkling here and there, always just clear of the slow forward pacing of the grazing animals. How immaculate these Wagtails were, quite worthy of prolonged inspection. The telescope revealed more—they were White Wagtails, and a cock Pied Wagtail looked small and dingy in their company. The colour contrasts on the White Wagtails were remarkably clear and well defined; deep black bib, beautiful grey back, creamy white face and cheeks, pale edges to wing coverts making a perfect little bird. Some of them came to the road and on to the flat-topped, lichened wall near the car window. Hither and thither they pecked and tumbled, sprites of fairy-like grace and lightness, and I could have watched them for hours had not W. suddenly drawn my attention to a solitary swan flying from the field pool. Solitary swans always had to be examined and this one looked smaller than a Mute Swan and, in flight, decidedly shorter in the tail. It swung round over the Cob and landed with a swish on the lake. The telescope revealed a young Bewick's Swan. Much of its plumage was still suffused with pale brown, but that part of its bill which was not black had changed from the juvenile dull-pink and was showing a dull yellow. As we watched it began to feed on the bottom of the lake, and for long periods its head and neck were under water. Later five young Mute Swans flew to the pool but the young migrant swan made no attempt to mix with them.

APRIL 17TH. This morning the five young Mute Swans and the solitary Bewick's Swan were still on Cob Lake, the Bewick still very much alone and again feeding. Two of the Mute Swans swam close together, necks very straight and upright, breasts often touching. While I watched they faced each other, curved their necks and dipped their heads. It almost seemed as if, in doing this, they stroked each others necks with their bills. This affectionate display was short lived, for another of the young swans, with plumes raised and neck laid back charged in and attacked one of the pair, reaching across the back of its victim and gripping its neck. It struggled and thrashed away from its attacker and was chased to wing,

21

Drakes Fighting

THE VILLAGE FROM THE COB

both birds flying for some yards before alighting with a spray-scattering rush. The chase was not continued, the attacking male returning to the other two swans with plumes still raised, and neck laid back between them. He was the whitest of the young swans, all the rest having much brown in their plumage, and none having any trace of the orange-yellow which marks the bill of the adult Mute Swan. I walked back home along the Cob and was in time to see three swans fly, leaving the other two, still swimming close together, on the water. I wonder if it is usual for swans to choose their life partners at such an early age? These two brown swans were not a year old

In the evening, during a walk along the estuary side we watched a piping party of three Oystercatchers, which would not have been particularily worthy of note had not the birds been belly-deep in the river. Sometimes in line abreast, sometimes in single file, and often all facing towards a centre, the piping went on, the river washing their flanks. With hardly any interruption to the performance they came on to the sandy shore where the excitement grew until one bird flew at another. Then there was more piping and more excited flying chases. We continued our walk and the three birds were still at it when we were half a mile away.

APRIL 18TH. The blackthorn has opened and the dark hedges are enlivened by its delicate blossom. Along some of the lanes there are whole hedges of it and here the effect of the blossoming is enchanting. But this evening the snow of its flowers has been joined by real snow brought by a cold north wind, and when we came to a halt by Cob Lake another squally storm of snow, sleet, and strong wind smote us.

Over the water of the lake a flock of Swallows flew low, and through the whirling flakes which were driven almost horizontally by the wind, we saw that they were feeding. Intermittently one or other of the flock lowered its head to the hissing surface and took something from it. I do not think they were drinking for their manner was too deliberate, and the pecking at the water-surface regular and without the tiniest splash. Heads to wind they hunted

22

SWALLOWS AND SAND-MARTINS

until they reached the head of the lake, then they lifted and allowed themselves to be whirled back until they were again over the middle of the expanse, where they once more turned head to wind and began their concentrated search and frequent delicate pecks at the surface. At length the snowstorm passed towards the mainland mountains, the wind abated and the sun shone. The Swallows lifted from their labours and all flew to the flat coping of the low roadside wall just behind the car—perhaps ten feet away from us. Never was seen a more charming company; thirty Swallows and two Sand-martins on the orange-lichened grey wall lit by the evening sun. They rested for a few minutes, then were away over the lake, this time to hunt high.

While watching the Swallows we had caught a glimpse of a sunlit flock of birds swooping down to a field farther along the road so, as much will have more, thither we went, and saw that the recently harrowed field held a flock of Golden Plover. Golden they were, but also very black and white, a flock of approximately four hundred birds, all of the Northern race. The most immaculate of them appeared as black birds each clothed with a white-edged golden shawl which fitted over the head and fell behind the cheek to be brought forward and loosely fastened down the breast, thence to flare away along the sides. Perhaps more than half were thus attired, the others, though most had the white edge to the shawl, had brown or pale buff cheeks and some white feathers spotting the black breast. W. and I agreed that the Northern Golden Plover in breeding plumage is in the topmost rank of well-dressed birds.

On the field there were two pairs of resident Lapwings, and the cock birds, between the occupations of making scrapes in the brown earth, and displaying to their hens, flew playfully above their Golden cousins and, stooping here and there, caused individuals to crouch or take wing; or again a Lapwing would suddenly run in where the flock of Goldens was thickest and menace whichever bird was nearest to him putting one after another to flight. Compared with the quick sharp-winged Northerns the Lapwings looked big and clumsy, with their broad-ended wings beating once where those of the Goldens flickered three or four times.

When the nearest birds were so close to the road that they were out of the focus of my telescope a passing bus caused the whole flock to take wing and we thought that this was the end of our watching. The birds wheeled about the confines of the field in ever-changing formation, one part of the flock at times seeming to pour down through the other. One moment golden backs only were to be seen, the next the silver and black undersides. Soon it became obvious that the plover were reluctant to leave the field, and after several undecided swoops almost to ground level the whole flock wheeled and came round heads to wind. On set wings they glided down, then, with a silvery flickering of wings beautiful to watch the host ceased its forward progress and delicately touched ground, the last birds to alight flashing this way

23

NORTHERN GOLDEN PLOVER ALIGHTING

and that to avoid a landing on the backs of those below. When all wings were closed the compact group of birds was almost invisible against the brown earth, except for those white fringes to their shawls which gleamed like a series of white question marks. Twice more they were put to wing, once by two dogs and again by a passing motor lorry, but each time they returned to the same spot with the same exquisite manœuvre.

We gazed and gazed on this immaculate congregation knowing well that this was a feast that might not occur again for another twelve months, and at last, with many regrets, we left them to their brown field and the night.

APRIL 19TH. A boisterous wind roared up the estuary this evening, and the windows in the front of the house creaked as they took the onslaught of the gale. We decided to have a quick look at the field pools and Cob Lake and got out the car, for in this sort of weather the car is by far the best observation post. At once we saw that the vicinity of the field pools was alive with small birds. Swallows and Sand-martins were flying low over the wind-swept water, heedless of the gale, and on the grassy flats White Wagtails were everywhere, some feeding on the grass, others seeking shelter under the foot-high edge of the pool. It was while we were watching the bird traffic that the glasses rested upon a spot of bright yellow at the edge of the pool. I saw that it was a cock Yellow Wagtail, very exquisite and vivid even as he huddled in the earth bank. Later he moved up on to the grass and hunted with his White cousins, and it was interesting to note how much smaller he was when compared with them.

We moved on a few yards and looked at Cob Lake where a grassy peninsular juts into its length. At the edge of the grass a Redshank had just commenced the " butterfly " display behind a hen bird, but the wind was so strong that when the bird began to vibrate its wings it was lifted at once into the air, without any preliminaries on the ground.

On the lake Shelduck in pairs rode the wavelets, serene and immaculate, sometimes forgetting their dignity to up-end and feed on the bottom of the shallows.

We returned to the field pools and, pulling up very close to the wall, saw that there were White Wagtails only a few feet away from it. Gusts blew their feathers awry, and tails were disarranged, but they continued their quest for food among the tumps of grass growing from the swamp. With them were Meadow-pipits, and then W. discovered the Reed-buntings—two of them, one a young cock bird, the other an adult cock in the most flawless plumage I have ever seen on any bird. He was unbelievably smart and handsome and no words could truly

24

YELLOW WAGTAIL, REED-BUNTING AND WHITE WAGTAIL

convey the effect of his black head and bib against his white collar and striped back. Both birds were with the company under the wall, only a few feet away.

Out in the water a small party of Redshanks were feeding and, near them, two other larger birds had arrived while we had been delighting in the buntings. The telescope identified a pair of Black-tailed Godwits in breeding plumage. One, the more handsome of the pair, was noticeably smaller than the other, and this I assumed to be the male. He was handsome even at a distance, and the glass revealed his cinnamon head, neck and chest, and the black bars on his white flanks. His lady was much quieter in her colours. Both birds kept close together and hunted industriously, sometimes wading so deep that they appeared to be swimming. The whole of their heads and necks were often submerged. They were still feeding when we came away. Wind was becoming still stronger and a rough night was almost a certainty.

APRIL 20TH. Blowing a gale all day, sometimes with heavy rain. In the evening the sky in the west cleared and the sun shone, but the strength of the wind did not abate. We took the car along to Cob Lake, but there were only swans riding its little waves; nothing on the field pools and only the White Wagtails sheltering below the shore line of the grass. By the field pool of Bont Farm a solitary swan grazed and this we found to be an adult Bewick's Swan. It was engrossed in its feeding and plucked at the grass hungrily, heeding nothing. We watched and noted the peculiar S-curve of its neck while grazing. Out of the water the Bewick's Swan looked a strong stocky bird with thick black legs.

We returned to the swans on Cob Lake. Five of them were Mute Swans, but there were four others which kept apart. If they were Bewick's why did not the other swan join

25

BLACK-TAILED GODWITS

them? Prolonged scrutiny in the difficult light and strong wind revealed that they were Whooper Swans—two adults and two young. They rocked gracefully on the rough water, and fed with heads and necks under water, their beautifully shaped backs wet and gleaming in the evening sun. Sometimes they swam together and, if the wind was on their flanks, each bird inclined its neck into the wind to lessen resistance. But the typical straight necked position was not in evidence this evening, and usually necks were curved gracefully. When they preened the sun revealed, in the modelling of their necks, the position of each bone, a feature I have not noticed in the plumper-necked Mutes. The wind shook the car so violently and made observation so difficult that we decided home was the best place.

BEWICK'S SWAN GRAZING

26

April 21st. A howling gale blowing all day with one of the highest tides of the year. At midday waves were breaking under the garden wall, to shoot up in spray over the roofs of the little cottages by the wall. By the end cottage the sea wall is not very high, and the waves frequently broke over its coping, so that geese in the yard were paddling in pools of salt water. On the bastion at the end of the Cob waves were hammering and bursting up in great gouts of spray which scattered over the road; and the little lane with its opening to the beach was awash. A wild and disturbing day!

April 22nd. Sometime during the night the wind abated its fury to, perhaps, half a gale so that, at midday to-day, the high tide did not strike the garden wall with such a threatening thud as yesterday, though the waves in the estuary were still considerable, and spray was flying over the lawn and the cottages again. W. had been watching the tide from the lounge window when she suddenly cried out " Terns." I grabbed glasses and joined her, and saw, where the waves were flooding over a bed of dark brown rushes a few yards from the garden wall, two terns hovering heads to wind and feeding. From their hover, a yard above the water, they would suddenly dip to pick up some tiny morsel from the crest or the trough of the waves—a pretty manœuvre in which the birds did not make the smallest of splashes. Long wings and tail streamers were constantly adjusted to the buffets of the wind, and it was a marvel how the fragile creatures kept their station above their chosen area. For many minutes they dipped and flickered, constantly feeding, then, without effort, rose almost vertically and let the south-west wind blow them over the house top, over the village, and out of sight.

Later I saw three terns resting on the grassy verge of the field pools in company with Redshanks and White Wagtails, and later still in the evening, we counted seventeen terns over Cob Lake intent on their feeding. Food appeared plentiful, for the terns constantly dropped to the water surface and often submerged head and neck, making a pronounced splash before beating up into the wind again. Below them, Shelduck in pairs, and a solitary Bewick's Swan swam and fed, unheeding this first appearance of the terns. But, to us, it was a real sign of spring, though spring is late in coming to Anglesey this year; hawthorn hedges are still dark with the merest sign of green, and gorse is late in flowering.

TERNS BY THE GARDEN WALL

SOUTH-WEST GALE

APRIL 23RD. A dreadful day! Winds which threatened to blow everything across the island and a high tide at noon, made all other gales we have experienced here seem infantile. At its height great spouts of spray came over the garden wall, sometimes in solid jets, at others in wide clouds of fine spray which enveloped the end of the nearest little cottage, the yard of which was awash. On the lawn a wide pool developed, and another on the drive, both of which were caused by spray and not rain. We were pleased when " high tide " was past but, owing to the following south-west gale, it was several hours before the sand of the estuary became uncovered. Across the wet expanse the swollen river rolled, and, to-day, the lovely S-bend was obscured by the brown flood water.

In the evening I went along the road between the field pools and Cob Lake. Over both sheets of water terns were feeding. Their numbers had increased considerably since yesterday, and in the two companies, there must have been about sixty birds. To-night it was a real fairy ballet, elegant performance of dipping, soaring, flickering dancers, with the hissing waves as their stage and a scurrying wind-torn sky as backcloth.

In complete contrast a cormorant splashed up from Cob Lake and flew low over the water until, rising to clear the Cob, he met the full force of the gale, and then, unable to cope with the shrieking wind, was blown back, and landed on the lake again, a ragged heavy black shape. He dived as if ashamed.

APRIL 24TH. The sun shone all day to-day, and although the wind was still strong it had lost that dangerous, threatening roar. Until the evening I had to content myself with glances at the glistening estuary through the studio window. When the incoming tide had reached and covered the bed of rushes near the garden wall two terns came there to feed just as I had seen them on their first appearance. This evening as I went into the lounge, I saw, perched

28

Northern Golden Plover

on the garden wall, four feet from the window, a cock and hen Yellow Hammer. They flitted from there to the bramble tangle, and my hope is that they will nest there. Our Stonechats of the first few days have not returned.

Seven o'clock, summer-time, found W. and I at the end of the little lane, arched with its canopy of wind-bent trees, which opens on to the Menai Straits exactly opposite Caernarvon Castle. It was low tide and sand-bank and shingle were uncovered. Seen through the frame made by the hedge and the arch of the trees the castle and the mountains made an enchanting picture which we admired at length. Here is the place where, it is said, the gentry used to cross in their carriages, after the farmers and the peasants had laid down a causeway of loads of wood, from the island shore to Caernarvon.

Birds had not been in our thoughts until we saw a movement on the shingle below us. Our glasses found three Whimbrel, uneasy at our presence, but not inclined to leave. The telescope made clear their trim bodies and beautifully laced plumage, as well as the light eye stripe and dark, curved bill. They allowed us five minutes in which to watch them, then fled westwards down the straits.

On the way home we pulled up by Cob Lake, and focussed glasses and telescope on a tern which was resting on the grassy shore. Up to now the terns had been on the wing in a strong wind, and identification had been difficult, but now there was no doubt of this one. Its completely red bill told us it was an Arctic Tern. Possibly all the others were of this species and storm-driven while on passage. A number were feeding over the lake but not so many as on the previous evening.

CAERNARVON FROM ANGLESEY

APRIL 28TH. Early this morning, as I was watching the sunlight on the sand and the river, a Cuckoo called, and as this was the first time of hearing him this year, I dutifully " turned my money over." All day the sunlight sparkled on the curve of the river, and the Rivals loomed in the background dusky blue and shapely. The six white geese from the cottages splashed and capered about in the water, and created a great clamour as the gander mated with one of the geese. But there was work to be done, and the time-devouring gazing through the studio window had to cease.

In the evening W. and I went to our usual roadside station between Cob Lake and field pool, and watched the dance of the terns as they plunged, and floated up, and plunged again, tireless wings beating, tail streamers constantly adjusted, watchful heads down-bent to the

29

water of Cob Lake. Again, in the shallows of field pool, a solitary Ruff was seen in company with Redshank and near a pair of dazzling Shelduck. The Ruff was at the far end of the water and both W. and I had focused our glasses on him when a nearer grey shape floated into the field of the lenses. Simultaneously we said "Harrier!" In a second glasses were refocused and the bird with the pale-grey, down-bent head, long, flexible, black-tipped wings with a dark bar on the grey of each, was identified as a male Montagu's Harrier. For a time he hunted over the rushy pasture. He glided, floated, banked, hovered, and sometimes rocked on those graceful up-tilted wings, gradually working his way to the shore. He allowed the breeze to take him, drifting low over the water, not more than a yard above Shelduck and Redshank. All ignored him, except one Shelduck, which thought fit to bow as he went over her. Effortlessly he soared, hesitated and scrutinised the road for a second, then began a systematic hunt of the rushes by Cob Lake. Here he had a little clash with the Arctic Terns, two of them mobbing him and causing him to tower. There were no collisions, the Harrier

ARCTIC TERNS OVER COB LAKE

easily avoiding the exuberant dives of the terns. Then two Black-headed Gulls made an attack. They were more persistent than the terns, but the Harrier, with a quick flick of his wings, slipped sideways and the gulls went sailing past, yards away from their objective. The Harrier was now over the Cob and against the background of dunes and the Rivals. He hunted the length of the Cob almost up to the village, then we saw him slip away in the direction of the rushes under our garden wall and I was wishing that I could be transported to the studio that instant. But now the Cob hid him and we did not see him again. So we contented ourselves with the White Wagtails which were now perched on the roadside walls and on the road itself. One moment they would be on the lichened coping, the next on a projecting stone out of sight only to bob up again on the coping a yard farther on. Needle-sharp black eyes set in the middle of cream-white faces regarded us curiously before the dainty creatures passed on along the stones. Cuckoos, Harriers, hawthorn hedges at last breaking into green. and the blackthorn in bloom, surely real spring will be with us soon!

HARRIER CROSSING FROM FIELD POOL TO COB LAKE

APRIL 29TH. The road from the village, after crossing the river, traverses the mile-wide marsh and then winds upwards through the sand-hills. Here its margin is marked by white-painted pyramidal stones and these also mark the place from which there is a fine prospect. One can survey a little damp gully in the dunes below where grow young flag iris, a long bed of bright green horsetail, a few small sallow bushes, and patches of rush. Around its edge grows dwarf willow. The gulley ends in a pool in a hollow of marram-covered sand-dunes, and beyond stretch the saltings and the estuary, and then the rising ground of fields and woods dotted here and there with farms and cottages of grey stone.

WHEATEAR DISPLAY

31

STONECHAT PAIR

Within one minute of our arrival a cock Wheatear flashed into view and perched on the tip of a dead ragwort stalk, soon to be followed by a hen bird which came to rest in a hollow in the sand. The cock bird flew down to her, and immediately began to perform the strangest antics in front of the hen which stood very still and erect. He flashed first to one side and then to the other across her front with a great show of open tail, and after perhaps thirty seconds of this half flying, half leaping, crouched before her with tail fully open and slightly raised, at the same time vibrating his wings laterally and so rapidly that their shape was just a blur. The hen made a sudden move away from him and his posturing and displaying came to an abrupt end. He, as if impatient with her, streaked away across the dunes, and she ran and bounced about the sand-hill, hunting for food, and at times perched on the old grey ragwort stalks.

Other birds had a fondness for these old stalks as perches, especially a pair of Stonechats which, as if filled with curiosity, had crossed the road, resting first on the top of the white stones near us, and then on to the ragwort stems below us. The hen appeared first and, after perching on a bleached stalk for several seconds, during which she constantly opened and closed her tail, he dropped to the ground and hunted. Soon she had found a large fat caterpillar and, with this held in her beak, flew rapidly up the gulley. She was soon back again, and another caterpillar was found and taken away. She was very beautiful, but when the cock appeared he was, by contrast, strikingly so, for I had never seen a Stonechat with a wider white collar nor a brigher cinnamon-brown breast. When he perched on the topmost twig of a new-leafed sallow, the combination of fresh green and brown, black, and white was a perfect one. He was not so industrious a parent as his mate and once, when he found an extra fat caterpillar, he could not resist it and swallowed it himself. While memory was fresh Wheatear and Stonechat notes were made in the sketch-book but, ere long, a brown shape crossing the dunes compelled me to exchange book and pencil for field-glasses.

The sharp-winged shape alighted at the far edge of the pool under the sand-dunes and, when it turned its breast to the water, I could see that it was a Merlin. For a while, it stood by the pool side and gazed around with large, dark eyes. Then, leisurely it stooped to drink. It sipped, then pointed its bill skywards, sipped again, and again raised its bill like any drinking farmyard hen. It seemed very thirsty. Presently it walked deeper into the water and, with quick movements of head, threw showers of spray over back and shoulders. Then wings were brought into play and, with vigorous shakes

32

LAPWING MOBBING MERLIN

and thrashings, more showers were splashed over back and tail.

While the Merlin was bathing a Moorhen skulked through the rushes and dwarf willow of the opposite side, and took to the water, swimming directly towards the Merlin. As the distance between the two birds lessened the Moorhen puffed out its neck, stretched it along the water and looked most menacing. The Merlin carried on with its toilet and completely ignored the Moorhen which, when it found that its show of fierceness had no effect, swam back to the rushes, its neck still puffed out.

The Merlin, which was a female, gazed calmly about her, and then flew to the cornice of a high sand-dune where she shook herself and preened. Suddenly a Lapwing appeared from nowhere and stooped at the Merlin which dipped as the Lapwing flashed over. Again and again the angry, calling bird dived, wide wings hissing as it swished up after almost grazing the back of the Merlin. After suffering several more of these mad stoops the hawk left the dune, still attended by the frantic Lapwing which, in the air, was powerless to touch the nimble " side stepping " falcon. Soon the Lapwing gave up the chase leaving the Merlin to preen in peace on a more distant dune.

No sooner had this affair ended than another Lapwing hullaballoo was heard among the dunes in the opposite direction. Above the crests of marram grass Lapwings could be seen intermittently as they pitched up, to stoop again at something behind the dunes. Soon a great black bird came flapping over a sand-hill and landed just below the top of the ridge. Four screaming Lapwings swooped and swished about it, and with good reason, for the bird was a Raven and in its bill it held an egg. The black raider ducked as the Lapwings came at him, but soon decided that that particular corner was too hot for him and resumed his flight over the dunes, swinging and shifting to avoid the enraged birds, the egg still held in his bill. That chase was carried to a great distance, and the progress of the Raven, though not seen, could be guessed by the high screaming of the Lapwings.

Just before noon gulls came to the pool to bathe. First a huge Black-backed Gull sailed down and came to rest on the water as lightly as one of his own snowy breast feathers might have done. Herring Gulls followed, and with them three Lesser Black-backed Gulls. Then what a splashing and a thrashing disturbed the pool; what a dipping of heads and a rolling of bodies first to one side and then the other; and what fine showers of spray burst up from

RAVEN MOBBED BY LAPWINGS

33

Montagu's Harrier and Arctic Terns

POOL IN THE DUNES

beating flights and side-shaking tails! It was a sparkling, animated scene of pleasure and intense enjoyment. As the gulls left the pool and gained height each one indulged in a vigorous shaking in mid-air before sailing away to the estuary, accompanied often by the irate Lapwings.

Soon after one o'clock, just as we were finishing lunch, a great piping was heard in the sky above the house. We dashed to the door and saw a flock of Golden Plover wheeling and turning above the village and the house. The field-glasses revealed the jet black of their breasts and throats, and we surmised that possibly they were the same flock of Northern Golden Plover which had delighted us on the evening of April 18th, and on several occasions, on the same ploughed field, since that date. As they circled they appeared to gain height, then suddenly a small group broke away from the main flock, and setting a course slightly west of north they flew in formation, which sometimes was in the form of a V and at others became a crescent, direct and purposeful until lost to sight beyond the hill of Bodorgan. At intervals of a few seconds other small groups left the main flock and headed away in the same direction, until the whole congregation, in small formations, one behind the other, was making its way northward. Their piping became fainter and fainter and then was heard no more. We were sorry to see them go for they were birds of great beauty and charm.

But as some birds depart others arrive. The flock of White Wagtails has increased and so has the number of Swallows and Sand-martins hunting Cob Lake. On several occasions there have been seen on the sands large flocks of Redshanks, and I can only think that these, too, are migratory, for the resident population seems to have split up into pairs and only occasionally does it gather into small groups.

APRIL 30TH. When we watched the Golden Plover depart yesterday we had hoped that it was a sign that spring would soon be with us. But this morning a cold north wind blew down the garden and howled about the chimneys, a full-throated winter blast which must have brought snow with it, for, as the clouds cleared from the mountains, Snowdon and its smaller outpost Yr Aran gleamed pure white.

On the river, in front of the house, six ducks swam in a compact group but when two Herring Gulls swooped down at them they took wing—six belated Wigeon, four of them

34

drakes. They made off over the Cob and swung up the marsh in a north-easterly direction. Perhaps they too were migrants from a more southerly place and were on their way to their northern breeding grounds. Our local winter Wigeon have usually left by the first week in April.

The cold wind blew all day, and there was little inducement to leave the studio, but in the evening W. and I visited Cob Lake. We found that some of the Arctic Terns had departed for there were only a dozen birds hunting the grey, wind-whipped water. Below them five young Mute Swans breasted the little waves, and a Cormorant suddenly surfaced with a large eel gripped in its bill. The eel thrashed this way and that, twisting and curving convulsively, sometimes round the bill and head of its captor. Slowly the Cormorant shifted its grip until it had the eel by the head, then with a quick jerk, started to swallow the fish head first. Perhaps half of its length had disappeared when there were more violent struggles and the eel backed out and again was held only by the head. But the grim, hooked beak held and the eel was now dipped in the water. After a rest of a few seconds the Cormorant began to gulp and jerk the fish into its gullet. Soon only three inches of the tail remained projecting from the side of the bill, and, with a final gulp, this too disappeared. The Cormorant, with long, bulging, mishapen neck, rested awhile, then the bulges in the neck moved suddenly and again three inches of the eel's tail projected from the side of the beak. But it was a losing battle for the eel and gradually it was quite engulfed and the Cormorant's neck regained its normal sinuous contours. The bird drank then dived again.

Turning to the field pool we spied " him " questing the rough ground near Bont Farm, " him " being our term for the cock Montagu's Harrier. He was soon pestered by the ever-present Lapwings and, to-night, they seemed to be more aggressive than usual for a pair set about him and forced him to whirl this way and that, once causing him to shoot up vertically, then, to avoid the stoop of a second Lapwing, to turn on his back and to spiral down in a mad tumble almost to the level of the pool. When he was left in peace he hunted the rushes and

CORMORANT WITH AN EEL

35

gorsey patches, sometimes almost dropping to the ground, then suddenly changing his mind and continuing his quest on those wonderful up-tilted wings, up the marsh and beyond the railway embankment behind which he disappeared.

As we turned to go home two Common Sandpipers arrived by the grassy edge of Cob Lake—the first Sandpipers we have seen this year.

HARRIER HUNTING BY BONT FARM FIELD POOL

SHELDUCK CHASING SHOVELER

MAY

MAY 1st. Over Cob Lake to-night there hovered but two terns. As usual they fished diligently and tirelessly. A pair of Shoveler duck swam in the middle of the lake, and I was about to focus the telescope on the drake when a Shelduck lifted from the water and flew the thirty yards or so which separated him from the Shovelers. He flew straight at them and they took wing and sped up the lake with the Shelduck after them. He gained on them and almost touched the Shoveler drake which made a sudden swoop up, the Shelduck on his tail. The pursuit was not prolonged, the Shelduck returning to his mate, and the Shovelers to another part of the water. Not more than thirty seconds elapsed before another Shelduck took up the attack, and again the Shovelers were forced to flee. This time they were chased across the road and came down on Bont Farm pool. Here another Shelduck objected to their presence, and the Shovelers were once more in the air, chased by this large, pied, scarlet-nebbed demon. Whichever water the Shovelers rested upon they were, at once, attacked. These flights were most exhilarating to watch. The pied plumage of the drakes flashed in the golden evening sunlight against the background of marsh, Cob and village, and sometimes against the great mountains whose snow-covered shoulders loomed into the clouds in the south-eastern sky. At length, after making many circuits of the waters, and many crossings of the road, the Shovelers alighted near the bank of Bont Farm pool, and swam into the shore where a little bay partly concealed them. But they had been seen, for a Shelduck began to swim towards them. Both Shovelers' heads sank below the low bank, and the Shelduck, losing sight of his quarry, turned back to his mate. In the sanctuary of their little bay the Shovelers rested, the drake immediately tucking his bill in scapulars and going to sleep as if tired out, while his duck preened vigorously.

37

SHOVELER PAIR

Another pair of Shovelers, on farmyard field pool, fed quietly and unmolested in the company of five swans and two herons. (These herons, at this time, are in the most perfect plumage.) This particular pair of Shovelers has been on farmyard pool several weeks and deserves to be watched.

MAY 2ND. " The north wind doth blow and we shall have snow." More correctly, a nor'-easter doth blow, and during a brief glimpse of Snowdon it was clear that more snow had fallen in the mountains for his shoulders and peak were pure, unbroken white.

This evening, on my walk to Cob Lake, I found terns flickering over the farther reach. They were newcomers, much smaller than the Arctic Terns, and a closer approach revealed the white foreheads, yellow, black-tipped bills, and the short tails of Little Terns. Their wing beats were quicker, more butterfly-like when compared with the slow, flexible strokes of the Arctic Terns. Before I arrived at the point at which the Little Terns had been hovering and wheeling all but two had disappeared. At this farther point of the lake a grassy peninsula projects from the road into the lake and towards the Cob, this intrusion making a narrow neck of water with wider areas on either side of it. I sat by the roadside and watched the two terns, and presently they also disappeared under the lee of the foot-high bank of the peninsula farthest away from me. So there was nothing for it but to brave the bitter wind, and gain the top of the Cob. A walk along the road, and a stepping-stone crossing of swampy ground between road and Cob, brought me to the base of the Cob. I climbed its sloping side and was glad to drop down on the other more sheltered slope which breasts the open estuary. A short return walk, a climb to the top of the Cob, and a peep over the top, brought me opposite to, and into a good observation place for, the terns. Now they were all huddled under the low bank, and resting on a recently uncovered spit of mud, eleven Little Terns in company with as many Redshanks, four Dunlin, and a pair of Shelduck. The terns rested in a line, all heads to wind, and dotted along the mud like a string of pearls. They remained thus for perhaps five minutes, then one stretched its wings vertically above its back, and flew off to the water. Two others, with the same upward wing stretch, soon joined the first, and unhurriedly, by ones and twos, all the others took wing, until the whole company was fishing again. With flicker and splash they fed, heedless of the roaring north-easter, while I could hardly keep glasses steady, and was soon glad to drop down on the sheltered side of the Cob, and make my way home.

There were no Arctic Terns to be seen this evening, either over Cob Lake or the field pools, and it was interesting to note that this first appearance of the Little Terns was one day later than their arrival last year.

LITTLE TERNS

MAY 3RD. A day of many changes. This morning the wind was still in the north-east, but by the evening, it had swung to the south and the air was warm. Never had the estuary looked more lovely with the sands dark sepia and the river a shining steel-blue curve one minute, the next, tawny stretches with the winding blue water deeper in tone than the sands; mountains visible and then lost in cloud. All morning a flock of migrant Dunlin, of perhaps a hundred birds, fed on the sand and often flew in close formation, winding this way and that, to return to their original feeding ground. At one time they were joined by the Little Terns, but these, having come to the sands for rest and not food, remained quiet and separated from the busy Dunlin, who ran about, hither and thither, like mice.

The evening was so glorious that we could not stay indoors. Great clouds were piled above the mountains, now clear cut and in definite light and shade their snows gleaming in the sun. First we went along to the end of the Cob and searched with the glasses, hoping to see the Harrier, but his pale-grey shape did not appear over the sunlit dunes, nor in front of the ridge with its tiny farmhouses and fields. But, as we watched, two dark, sharp-winged birds came striding through the air above the sand-hills, and we saw that they were Swifts. They sped over the saltings and the Cob, and did not linger. They were flying due north. To the east a rainbow shone against a dark thundercloud which had slowly formed among the mountains and which now enveloped them completely. Against this dark blue cloud the nearer landscape blazed with yellow light, and the shadows of gables and house-sides were almost black and very distinct. On came the cloud, and, as we checked to watch its progress

39

WHIMBREL ARRIVING OVER COB LAKE

across the vista of marsh, the first heavy drops of rain hit the car. Bodorgan and the village were still sunlit when a flight of birds wheeled over the Cob and, after some manœuvring, moved down the lake in a close, dark formation and, after more turns and undecided flutterings, alighted on mud at the lower end. We turned and went back after them, and found them to be Whimbrel, a charming company of thirty-four. They preened on the mud spit under the shadow of the Cob, with Dunlin and Redshank for company.

The great cloud now filled the northern sky, its ragged edge stretched above the setting sun, and taking on a rosy glow from it. That part of the sky which was clear was a pale " duck egg " blue, and while we admired all this and the reflections in the lake, the Whimbrel suddenly took flight and, after splitting into two groups, raced away over the tide-covered estuary. Then, high up, we saw a hawk and, dodging and side-slipping before it, a tiny bird silhouette. Many times the hawk made an effort to come up with the little bird, but always it was a fraction too quick, and presently the hawk turned away as if to end the chase. He flew well away from his quarry, then, as if suddenly changing his mind, came hurtling back and made another determined attempt, and was again successfully dodged. Finally, giving up the pursuit, he dived behind the Cob and was lost against

MERLIN CHASE

40

the shadowed hillside of Bodorgan. The hawk was a Merlin, slender and sharp-winged, but I failed to identify his intended victim. Both birds were seen only in dark silhouette against the luminous sky.

MAY 4TH. This Evening, with Wack and Margot, we went to the headland below Tyn Llewydan Farm, for we had heard rumours of Choughs having been seen, indeed, there were more than rumours, for a Chough had been found dead in a rabbit trap some time ago. The headland below the old grey farm is very wild; grey, rocky outcrops jut up from slopes which in summer are covered with bracken. This evening the first few crozier heads only were showing above the mosses and the ground ivy.

LESSER BLACK-BACKED GULLS

It is the kingdom of rabbits, stoats and weasels, of Kestrels and Wheatears, and nesting gulls. On Tyn Llewydan ground the Lesser Black-backed Gulls breed, and of this fact we became increasingly aware as we walked down towards the sea, for these fine upstanding gulls rested on the rough stone walls and the grey rocks, and stood in pairs about the rabbit-cropped sward. With them were Herring Gulls. Nesting had not really started in earnest, for the gulls were not unduly alarmed at our presence. There were plenty of nesting hollows but none of them contained eggs.

MALLARD DRAKES AT SEA

41

We came to a sandy bay enclosed by low rocky cliffs, and here we looked hopefully about us, but no black birds with red bills and legs were to be seen, only a few Jackdaws flew about the rocks. Oystercatchers flew off in alarm at our approach. What noisy birds they are—almost as nervous as Redshanks!

A party of duck riding the waves attracted our attention and we found that they were Mallard—a sea-going bachelor party, for all were drakes. Being accustomed to studying Mallard on the quieter waters of the Cheshire Meres I watched these sailors with renewed interest as they rode the waves, seemingly as much at home as any scoter.

A soft rain began to fall, as we retraced our steps up the sloping ground of Tyn Llewydan. A pair of Whinchats crossed our paths and, for a few moments, perched on dead bracken stalks, then were off and away.

We called at Tyn Llewydan where Mrs. Williams showed us a fine fox-skin which had been obtained as a result of a fox drive by farmers on the Caernarvon mainland. They, it seems, are pestered to desperation by foxes, and this skin was from a big fox, pale sandy in colour flecked with silver-grey along the back. If there are so many foxes on the Caernarvonshire lowlands one wonders how long it will be before they find their way across the straits and into Anglesey.

If Choughs had been in our thoughts, Peacocks certainly had not, for who would have expected to find these exotics on a wild Anglesey headland? Yet, at Trefri, our next calling place (Wack was determined to introduce us to as many people as possible this evening),

TREFRI

42

there were Peacocks pacing about the lawn in front of the ancient house, and Mr. Richard Owen was highly amused at our surprise. He is a breeder of pedigree Wiltshire sheep, and I think he was almost as proud of his Peacocks as of the many awards gained by his Wiltshires. The contrast of rocky and rabbit-infested headland with green lawns and Peacocks was great and unexpected. There was a certain elegant white Peacock, which I wanted to allude to as " she," so delicate did he look against his more gorgeous companions. We said " good night " to Mr. and Mrs. Owen and the Peacocks with reluctance, for Trefri was a pleasant place on that quiet evening.

SANDHILL POOL

MAY 6TH. Happening to glance from the studio window at the glittering tide, which had completely covered the sands, I caught a glimpse of a movement on the grassy shore beyond the garden wall. The " movement " strode up on to the grass in full view and so near that glasses were not required to identify it as a Whimbrel. It stood still for a minute, then walked neatly about the little saltings, pecking here and there; but the noises of the village were too close and soon it flew off over the shining tide, and was lost against the far dunes.

To-day the mountains have been at their best, clear-cut and in strong light and shade. Lines of snow still linger on Snowdon and the neighbouring heights, but no white broke the beautiful blue of the Rivals. All day they have loomed above the ever-changing estuary; sometimes a cloud has touched the sharp peaks of Yr Eifl and curled over the tops, but at no time had they been hidden.

In the evening we went to Newborough Pool which we found calm and without a ripple. This pool is by the dunes below Newborough village and is surrounded by reeds and other vegetation. Here the bog bean grows and it was in flower this evening. In time past this pool has been one of our happy hunting grounds and has harboured many birds. A pair of Shovelers among the bog bean, a pair of Tufted Duck in the middle of the pool, several Coot and Dabchick, was the sum of the visible bird population. The Shovelers were soon up and circling round; Tufteds, Coot and Dabchick all moved away by diving and swimming.

43

On its southern side the pool is flanked by a great expanse of sand-dunes which, in the evening light were beautiful against the background of the mountains. Here and there the hollows and pans of the sand-hills still retained the pools of winter, and the curves of little shores were echoed by the curves of the wind-sculptured dunes and their reflections. Creeping willow was everywhere, and where it grew thickly its pollen-covered catkins turned the dunes a lemon-yellow. Amongst it the rabbits and Lapwings looked exquisite, but a bird suddenly appeared amid a spray of it and the combination of bird and flowers completely took our breath away. This bird, a cock Wheatear, stood very upright, with tail half spread, breast towards us. He then bounced round and gave us a side view, tail still spread and brushing the sand. But it was when he turned his back to us that the full beauty of the tail was seen.

COCK WHEATEAR DISTRACTION DISPLAY   DISPLAY ON CREEPING WILLOW

Its flashing white fan was divided down the centre by black and its margin was black; the dark brown wings, folded above it became part of the black pattern, and the grey back and black facial stripe completed a colour scheme of the utmost elegance. When it flew it did so in strange laboured undulations and, when landing, it almost seemed to stagger for several feet, before regarding us again from its very upright stance. All the time, whether flying, running or standing, its beautiful tail remained expanded, and not once did we see the bird with its tail closed normally, though we watched it for a considerable time. Sometimes it uttered a wheezy note, almost like the wheeze of a Greenfinch. When it had enchanted us many times by perching on the tip of an upright, flower-covered stalk of willow, and on the very crest of a sand-dune amid stalks of marram grass, we came away. Possibly we were in the vicinity of the nest, on which his mate was sitting and all this fanning of the tail was but a " distraction display." For our part we were willing to be distracted by such beauty. Reluctantly we left it, with a feeling that if we caused it to hold its tail in that position much longer it would never more be able to close it.

STALLION PARADE

MAY 10TH. Hearing that there was to be a parade of Shire Stallions at Llangefni to-day, and being keen to revive old memories of similar parades in East Cheshire, W. and I went to town this afternoon, and found it full of people and cars. Farmers and their wives, sons and daughters were in the majority and the long main street was full of their quick Welsh speech. Some of the farmers were purposefully making their way up the hill which leads from the centre of the town so, following in their footsteps we came eventually to a field in which was a roped enclosure lined with spectators. Inside the ropes were the stallions and their grooms, and when we arrived a black stallion with white legs was showing his paces. Proudly he trotted down the centre of the enclosure, neck arched, " feathers " streaming, ribbons waving to his movements. At the ropes the groom turned him and trotted him back again, and at the far end came to a halt by the ropes. In the centre of the open space stood a man with a card, who, as the next stallion came down the grass, shouted out its name and other details of the animal. This stallion had fine action and, when it began to trot, there were exclamations of approval from the farmers. The stallion covered the course in grand style. Just as stylishly his little groom pranced by his side, and it was difficult to say which lifted knees the higher—stallion or groom. When the last stallion had shown his paces the crowd began to move from the field (which had for its background a rocky cliff on which stood the sail-less tower of an old windmill), and to return down the hill for the centre of the town. We followed and, at the bottom of the hill, waited. Presently the stallions came down the street with great swinging strides, their shining curves and decorated manes towering above the roofs of parked cars and the heads of the people. When they reached the clock tower in the square their grooms turned them sharply to the right. Here a last exhibition of their

45

COMMON TERNS

paces was given, and the trotting stallions swung round the bend, their powerful bodies slanting to the curve, and great hoofs ringing on the hard road. As they turned the corner they were hidden from sight, and, at once, the street was busy with moving people and cars. It was market day at Llangefni and the stalls appeared to be doing a roaring trade, from those which were selling cardboard boxes of chirping day-old chicks, to those selling all sorts of unnecessary gimcrackery. As the noises of car engines drowned the receding clop, clop, clop of the hoof beats and the occasional high neighing of the departing stallions, we made our way through the crowds and out of the town, glad to have seen a parade of " the great horse " again.

MAY 11TH. This morning two Common Terns rested on the grassy shore of Cob Lake—the first we have seen this season. As we watched they stretched their wings, and it was noticed that, in the backward and sideway stretching of the wing, they did not stretch a leg at the same time, as is the habit of many other birds, but kept them both firmly planted on the ground.

LITTLE TERNS: MALE POSTURING AFTER FEEDING FEMALE

46

RINGED PLOVER SHELTERING

Later in the day we were on the beach at Aberfraw. The tide was ebbing and the warm sun created clouds of vapour above the wet sand. At times this vapour was so opaque that it was difficult to see the curling breakers through it, and still more difficult to observe a party of birds which rested near the wave-edge. This party was made up of fourteen Oystercatchers, four immature Herring Gulls and two Little Terns. Of course it was the terns which retained our attention. Presently a passer-by disturbed the birds and, focusing glasses on the Little Terns, we watched one settle on the beach again, while the other flew over the waves. With bent head the flying bird searched the water and, hovering for a moment, suddenly dived like a Gannet, its impact with the water causing a tall splash. It did not quite submerge but flew up at once with a little gleaming fish held in its bill and made its way to the other tern resting on the beach. Alighting close by it the fisherman presented his catch to his mate (for this we assumed was the relationship). She took the fish and swallowed it while her mate postured for a moment with erect, extended neck and up-tilted bill, before taking off to resume his hunting. Soon he made another impetuous dive, and rose with another tiny fish, which he fondly presented to his mate, again indulging in the same momentary strange posture before leaving her. His dives were not always successful, but while we watched he must have fed his wife liberally, for he captured a fish every three or four minutes. More passers-by (the beach was a parade for the folk of Aberfraw) caused the terns to fly off but a party of Ringed Plover stayed, and dozed behind little heaps of seaweed on the smooth sand, and could hardly be seen amongst the dark spots of the weed. The reflected light from the bright sunlit sands transformed the passing gulls into wonderful gold-pink shapes, light against the deep blue of the sky.

MAY 12TH. At noon, happening to go out of the back door to watch a Linnet singing on the wall, a Sparrow-hawk came dashing over the garden in pursuit of a tiny bird which eluded it. All bird song ceased as the frustrated hawk soared in circles over the house without a wing-beat, a fine silhouette against a sky of midsummer blue. It was a large female. Finally it slid away below the line of the roof-ridge, and soon sparrows were chirping again in the privet hedge, and the crimson-breasted Linnet resumed his song from the top of a wind-torn poplar tree.

SPARROW-HAWK OVERHEAD

47

JACKDAW ON CHIMNEY-POT

MAY 16TH. During the last seven days the colour of Anglesey has changed from tentative scattered patches of spring green to full-leaved glory. In the fields the pretty Welsh lambs gambol among drifts of buttercups and daisies, and on the dunes the flashing cock Wheatears bob and curtsey amid sprays of creeping willow blossom, of white saxifrage, and purple ground ivy. But the gorse is only half hearted in its flowering, for the winter has left its mark and patches of dead brown separate the golden sprays.

Viewed from the studio window Common Terns, and less frequently Little Terns, have delighted us as they fished in the river or the tide, and daily Linnets and Greenfinches have come to the lawn to feed. Workmen repairing the chimney of the studio, have pulled out a half barrow-load of sticks and, with it, a full clutch of Jackdaws' eggs. No wonder I was suffocated with smoke on the one occasion I tried to light a fire! Another pair of Jackdaws is nesting in a chimney we do not use. The birds are always about the roof, but rarely pop down the chimney if they know that they are being watched.

Often during the past weeks our gaze has wandered to a sunlit white spot showing above the dunes to the south of the estuary, the top of the lighthouse on Llandwyn Island, and this evening Winifred and I set out, by way of Newborough, to reach that delightful place. From Newborough village a lane winds southwards and as it passes the old hilltop church there are wonderful views of the straits and the mainland mountains which fill the eastern and southern prospects. Past a few little stone farms it winds and then, dropping to the level of the dunes, the lane becomes a cart-track and then a path which, with difficulty, fights for its existence against the wind-driven sand of the dunes. Over hillocks of sand and marram grass and across flat pans, some of which still held considerable pools, we made our way until, at last, we came to the shore and the narrow causeway which connects the island of

LLANDWYN ISLAND FROM THE DUNES

Whimbrel

THE CORMORANT ROCK

Llandwyn to Anglesey. No need to use the raised causeway this evening for the tide was low and we crossed by the sandy beach to a cart-track which climbs up and across the island. Before we had gone far we stopped to admire the clusters of heartsease growing in lovely compact patches among the short grass. There were violets too, very deep in colour, growing with white saxifrage and purple ground ivy.

Near the ruins of the old church we met a donkey and a pony, vital connecting links between the dwellers on Llandwyn and their nearest supply base—Newborough. Both animals regarded us but refused to fraternise, the donkey turning away with a look of intense boredom, and the fat little pony refusing even a near approach. At the far side of the island there is a row of low, white cottages, a lighthouse, a derelict lifeboat house and some interesting rock scenery. This evening there was also Mrs. Jones, that sturdy old character who, in her young days, had helped to man the lifeboat, had acted as pilot to ships in the straits, and in her later years had broadcast about Llandwyn. We found her busy spring-cleaning, but in spite of this she was quite ready to talk at length on any subject connected with the " old place " —Llandwyn. We made ourselves known and told her we had come to live in Anglesey, and it transpired that she knew our new home well. Eventually she returned to her cleaning and we made our way to the beach, W. making for the places between the rocks where are to be found pockets of curious and beautiful shells, I to the lighthouse rock which commands a view of the Cormorant colony. From the high rock I focused the glasses on the islet where the Cormorants nest and saw that its upper surface was crowded with birds. The evening sun was shining directly into the glasses and the birds showed only as dark silhouettes against the brightness. In silhouette the necks of the nestlings could be seen reaching up to their parents' open bills for food, and the top of the rock was a mass of dark, sinuous shapes, some at rest, some preening, others feeding youngsters, while still other dark shapes took flight from, or alighted on, the crowded rock. Owing to the position of the sun no details could be observed, and soon I descended from the lighthouse and made for the low headland across the beach. W. was standing on the cliff-top by the White Beacon gazing through her glasses at passing birds. I joined her and she told me that there had been Roseate Terns over the water. I watched and, after closely examining several Common Terns, my glasses picked up one tern which was different, black of bill and with long tail streamers, which left no doubt as to the correctness of W.'s identification of the Roseates. Several times Roseate Terns passed and re-passed, and a Common Tern flying close by a Roseate looked dark-grey by

49

NORTHERN GOLDEN PLOVER

comparison. No pink was discernible on the breast of the Roseates, but this tint, at all times subtle and delicate, would not have been obvious at such a distance—from one to two hundred yards.

For a time we gazed at the terns and at the lovely hills across the straits, the rocky back-bone of Lleyn stretching away into the south-western sea, until the air, becoming cool and dew beginning to fall, we made our way from the beach. Saying a prolonged " good night " to Mrs. Jones, we joined the track, past the dark ruin of the old church and down to the causeway. Once more among the sandhills of the " mainland " we followed the tracks of a pony, which led us by easy ways through the high dunes and across the flat pans in a direction which we thought was the correct one. Presently we lost the pony tracks, and found ourselves well away from the line of telegraph poles which connect Llandwyn to Newborough, and so we had to strike across the dunes until the poles were once more in sight. But what a lucky chance had led us astray! We had not gone far when a bird moved on the stretch of creeping willow ahead of us and glasses revealed the most perfect Northern Golden Plover I have ever seen. This seeming perfection may have been emphasied by the fact that it was alone and amidst beautiful surroundings. We wondered why it was so belated, almost a month after the big flock which called on us in April. We watched this Northern bird for a long time for it did not fly, but moved when we moved and observed us from clumps of willow or heather. At length we dragged ourselves away and continued, ultimately to find our rough little lane and to climb with it to Newborough.

MAY 17TH. To-day our guest, John C., came in from his photographic activities with a story of a pair of Stonechats with a nest in the gorse bushes just along the shore, and that the cock had posed for him at a distance of a few feet, obligingly choosing the most flowery of gorse sprays on which to perch. So it seems that our Stonechats had not deserted us, but, after the great gales in April, had moved to a more sheltered spot farther along the shore.

50

MAY 20TH. A still, tranquil, hazy morning with pearly reflecting water and dreamy sunlight drew me from my work to the road by Cob Lake. On the lake four herons waited above four perfect reflections. Two of them were adults, the other two dark young birds of the season; almost certainly a family from the Bodorgan trees. The old Herons were aware of my scrutiny, and, one after the other, sprang to wing and beat strongly over the Cob. The two young birds were not so wary but lingered on the lake for a time. At last they, too, took flight, and it was noticeable that they had not yet attained their parents' confidence of wing for there was a faltering in their wing beats, as if they were not entirely sure of their balance, and they were much longer in settling necks back on shoulders and legs under tails than were the old birds.

Dotted about the mud and the grassy shore terns rested with heads tucked back and, on the spit which juts into the lake, there was a group of eight Common Terns, four Little Terns, a pair of Shelduck, five Redshanks, two Oystercatchers and three Black-headed Gulls. At the lower end of the lake terns were fishing and their splashes sent circles of ripples across the quiet water.

On the opposite side of the road the cattle from Bont Farm were standing in the mirror-like water of the field pool, their only movement an occasional swish of a tail, or a fly-ridding toss of a head. Among the cows a great Welsh Black Bull stood solid and majestic. Near them was another young Heron patiently peering into the water. Bont Farm itself was a hazy silhouette at the head of the pool, and the railway embankment beyond was lost in the distance of the marsh.

I walked along to the next field pool, to see if the Shoveler drake which, with his duck, had haunted this sheet of water since our arrival, was still there. The horsetails were growing but I could still see his immaculate shape above them and to-day there was another drake

ADULT AND YOUNG HERONS

51

with him. Both were among the horsetails and in front of a patch of flowering bog-bean. No artist could wish for more! The Shoveler duck was nowhere to be seen, but my search with the glasses revealed a tall-legged bird under the near shore—a Black-tailed Godwit. When a lorry went rattling along the road the Godwit tautened and lifted its head high, a fine athletic looking bird, but as the noise faded it relaxed and resumed its probing of the muddy shore and hoof-holes.

WELSH BLACK CATTLE ON BONT FARM POOL

MAY 22ND. The fine weather continues but I am tied to the studio, except for short dashes to the lake. This morning was bright and the mountains stood clear in the south without a cloud to break their grand contours. Cob Lake was noisy with the cries of gulls and terns, and, when I reached it, there was much activity among the birds, expecially those in the air, for Common Terns were fishing vigorously, plunging to the pool and having good hunting, judging by the excitement. Black-headed Gulls were behaving like terns, hovering and plunging and this morning, as frequently before, I thought that in the Black-headed Gull we have the connecting link between the gulls and the terns. The Black-heads were on the lake in numbers—most of them immature birds in very interesting plumages. Many had the complete sepia-brown head of the summer adults, while still showing some brown wing coverts and inner secondaries, and a very decided bar across the tail. Their bills and legs were dusky, and only the faintest tinge of maroon could be discerned on their bills. Among the flying birds there was sudden excitement when a tern stooped at a gull and chased it half the length of the lake, then the gull turned and chased the tern back again. Others joined in and soon there was an excited chasing up and down the lake which was obviously play and sheer joy in flying power. Tern chased gull, and gull chased tern and neither species

had any evil intentions towards the other. Excitement began to show among the gulls on the mud and pairs began to display, walking side by side, calling together with heads up, necks distended, wing shoulders out with flight tips crossed behind—another tern-like attitude. Often one would menace another crouching low, calling harshly, and approaching with slow deliberate stride. One pair of immature birds gave a most interesting exhibition; the more immaculate of the pair stood quite still while another, which had not attained the full " black " head, slowly walked in front of it, creeping low to touch the crop of the standing bird. Several times this happened,

IMMATURE BLACK-HEADED GULLS

the moving bird always brushing against the breast of the standing one and uttering a whining call as it did so. Suddenly the standing bird regurgitated a mass of food which the other at once swallowed—puzzling behaviour in immature birds.

MAY 27TH. Owing to the demands of work bird study has, for a week, been confined to the immediate vicinity of the house and garden, but it has not been without interest for all that. The bend of the river immediately in front of the studio window has attracted its gulls, terns, Cormorants, Redshanks and Oystercatchers, members of the last species having several times indulged in piping parties on the near shore. When the tide is at the full terns have a liking for a little area near the garden wall, and this same area at low tide, which then is a broken shore of grass, weed, rushes, and mud, has been haunted by a solitary Whimbrel for several days. A pair of Mute Swans come to the estuary at low tide, and they have thrilled me with flights from river to lake, often against the background of distant blue mountains.

On the front " lawn " Linnets descend to feed on dandelion seeds (of which there are woeful quantities), and Greenfinches come on the same errand. Two cock Stonechats dispute each other's right to perch on the garden shore-wall and there is invariably an attack should the two coincide on its lichened coping. In the garden at the back Goldfinches have arrived and there is often a pair of beauties in the hedge. In a rough corner of bramble and nettle the Willow-warbler still sings and chases other small birds from a particular perch in a gale-swept poplar tree. Only the Jackdaws are allowed to use this perch and this they often do. Their brood in the chimney has made its first flight but is still in residence, for we hear their squawks even when we are sitting in the kitchen, as the parents are still bringing food to the chimney.

One evening W. and I heard a Sedge-warbler stuttering away in the garden, but we did not catch sight of the bird. It was on this same evening, while I was pulling pea-sticks from a pile in a corner of the garden, that I suddenly came upon a Blackbird's nest with the hen bird still

FOOD-BEGGING

53

sitting and gazing at me with her dark bright eyes. I must have given her a shocking time, for I had not been gentle in handling the sticks, and the pile had rocked considerably. We stared at each other, then I began to replace the sticks above her until she was well concealed. She did not stir during the whole of the disturbance. Next day we saw that the nest contained four young.

A pair of Swallows sometimes haunt the roof of the house, flying round it and settling on the ridge. Why they hang about we cannot imagine for there are no desirable building sites available in roof or chimney. A pair of Great Tits have a brood in the stone wall of an outhouse and become very excited if one approaches too near the nest. The parents come to the little wall by the kitchen window and take their toll of the bread crumbs, often perching on the top of the pump handle or the head of the mop before descending to the flat stones on top of the wall.

Cuckoos put in sudden appearances, perch on post, tree, or wall for a few moments, then are off on their mysterious business again. Thrushes are sometimes seen though they are not plentiful. Those which come to the garden are doing good work judging by the piles of broken snail shells which surround certain stones. Perhaps the high spot was the visit of a Greater Spotted Woodpecker to the wind-stunted poplar tree in the garden. We were delighted to watch it as it searched the cracked and cankered bark for a time before swooping off and undulating over the village and out of sight.

WOODPECKER IN THE GARDEN

54

HERRING GULL TERRITORY

MAY 28TH. The morning was fine, and as I wanted to make drawings of Shags we decided that now was the time and Bodorgan headland the place, for we knew that they were nesting there. We left the car by the old wall above Bodowen Farm, and soon we were on the Warren, with the wailing, scolding gulls overhead, and the uncurling fronds of bracken at our feet. A green track winds down the sloping hillside, past rocky outcrops, and through a little valley on whose sides Herring Gulls were nesting. On the long boundary wall of the Bodorgan ground the gulls perched in lines and watched us pass. We came upon many nests and most of them contained eggs. (There were pellets about the nests and it was evident that the gulls had been feeding on late-sown corn, for the pellets were composed of the husks of oats.) Soon we reached the cliffs and the sandy bays, and I made my way to the Shags' nesting site while W. wandered off to explore elsewhere.

On the ledges of a steep cliff I found eight nests in full view and separated from me only by a narrow gully. I settled down to draw with Herring Gulls and their nests for company. My first Shag model had heaved itself up on its wing " shoulders " when I approached and, in this position, it remained for at least twenty minutes, regarding me with its gleaming green eye set like a jewel in its dark head. A white egg showed below its breast. While I drew she twisted her neck this way and that, one moment regarding me with her left eye, the next with her right. Completing the first drawing I started on my second model. This bird had its back towards me and when I made a move it protested with the weirdest noises, which sounded almost like the grunt of a pig. This bird had the largest crest of any in the colony, and was the only one to utter these unbird-like sounds. On one nest the parent bird was sitting peacefully when another Shag alighted a yard away from her. Out shot her neck in a vicious jab but she could not reach the newcomer which rested in an upright position, and remained unperturbed by this antagonism. Intermittently the bird on the nest shot out its neck to its fullest extent as if remembering that it was the thing to do.

The nesting activities were in all stages, one nest contained eggs, another the naked

55

NESTLING, FLEDGELING AND JUVENILE SHAGS

young, another the young in their grey down, and in yet another the young were half-fledged. But whatever their age the nestlings were queer gargoylish individuals with not one claim to be considered beautiful. Not so a fully-fledged bird which clambered about the ledges, for it was as shapely and sinuous as the adults. It was a brown bird, pale below, darker above, with a pale yellow eye.

Towards noon the sun was hot and some of the Shags, young and old, were gasping with their bills held open, but already rock shoulders were throwing shadows across them, and, by early afternoon, they would be in welcome shade. And so, having filled several pages with drawings, I left them and climbed the highest point of the headland to see if I could locate W. She was down on one of the sandy beaches so I made my way there. I had not gone far before I was mobbed by a particularly vicious Herring Gull. She came down at me like a dive-bomber and yelled a staccato, angry " keck! keck! keck! " at every stoop. She came at me from all sides, but her favourite line of attack was from behind when, if my eye was not on her, she would swish past uncomfortably close and cause me to bow respectfully. None of the other gulls attacked with the same vicious intentions as did this one. Her eggs were exceptional also for, besides two normally coloured ones, there was a pale blue one with scarcely any markings. I was thankful that the huge Great Black-backs, some of which nested on the highest headland near the Shags, had not adopted the same aggressive tactics. When I reached W. she told me that the same gull had attacked her, and had actually buffeted her on the head so that she had to carry a stick above her to divert the angry bird.

We had a most refreshing bathe in the little bay, then sat and watched a pair of Oyster-catchers which obviously had a nest close by. Cautiously, and as if anxious not to make a sound, one bird walked down the rocks, in a half-crouched attitude, until it reached the sand.

56

ANGRY HERRING GULL

Here it continued its stealthy progress right to the water's edge, and even into the water until it was belly-deep. But we remained seated and it flew to its mate on the rocks where both birds went into a furtive, crouching conference, as if discussing the next move. And the next move was an exact replica of the first—the stealthy crouching walk down the rocks; and so it went on until we left the bay. We joined the green track once more, and the gulls went with us right to the top of the Warren. When we looked back most of the gulls were settling on their nests again and the lower part of the Warren was closely dotted with brooding birds.

MAY 29TH. At four o'clock this afternoon we called at the school on the ridge, and picking up Wack and Margot we made our way to Holyhead, and beyond that strange place to the great cliffs of South Stack intent on Guillemots, Razorbills, and Puffins. When we arrived the fog signal was sounding, a sonorous full-throated note terminated by a deep thud which echoed along the cliffs and over the water into the mist. Later it cleared and the foghorn ceased, much to our relief. Leaving the car on the road we made our way down the headland to a point where we could see the rocky shelves on which the birds nested, and were not disappointed, for there they were in hundreds, making a nice compact little colony with Guillemots, as usual, crowded together, and Razorbills more exclusive and much less congested. My glasses wandered nearer, to a cliff on whose face wind and weather had worn a series of rough, huge steps. On these a garden of rock plants grew, especially sea-pinks and white campions, and it was while my glasses examined these colourful terraces that they came upon the grey-plumaged back of a bird, sitting cosily in a niche surrounded by sea-pinks. In great excitement I said, " I've got a Peregrine on its nest." W. and our two friends were all agog and presently found the patch of grey which was the bird. With the naked eye it was next to impossible to see it. I lost interest in Razorbills and Guillemots for the time being,

WORRIED OYSTERCATCHER

57

BROODING FALCON

and could hardly eat sandwiches because of the Peregrine. There she brooded (it was the Falcon if colour and size were any indication) with beak slightly open, unperturbed and even sleepy, for it was a very warm day and the sun was shining full on her. In my previous experience of Peregrines, the birds had always flown up and circled round calling shrilly, but with this bird there was none of that; she sat on, and roused only to raise herself and to make whatever it was under her more comfortable. She seemed to be turning eggs but we could not be sure. At long last I was dragged away to see close-ups of Razorbills and Guillemots and, from the steps which descend the cliff to the lighthouse there were some remarkable chances to study the birds intimately. Laying had not really begun yet for we saw but one egg, a beautiful blue one by the side of a Guillemot. But all the time I was thinking of the Peregrine and presently, after watching Puffins swimming below, we returned and Wack and I went down the headland to our vantage point for another look. The falcon still sat there with hardly any change in her position. Reluctantly I said good night to the quietest Peregrine I had ever met and vowed to return soon.

TIERCEL BROODING

JUNE

JUNE 1ST. Soon after three o'clock this afternoon W. and I were again on the cliff top at South Stack armed with a telescope as well as field-glasses. There was a Peregrine, but this time it was a smaller and a bluer bird that was brooding, obviously the Tiercel—male. He sat with his head pointing to the sea and his tail against the rock and, but for a casual, occasional glance, was no more worried by our presence than was the falcon on our previous visit. The tiercel brooded and appeared to be resting on wings which were lowered and held away from the body. Sometimes he bent his head and, by his movements, I suspected that he was covering young. At short intervals the bird raised itself slightly to shuffle down into an easier position. The telescope revealed every lovely detail of head, back, and fore-wing. After we had been watching some time I caught a glimpse of a dark shape flashing into the cliff and, moving the glass, saw the falcon swoop up and perch six feet from the nest on a shoulder of rock on which sea-pink and white campion were blooming. She looked wonderful in her wild garden; her trim, strong shape with its spotted chest, barred breast and flanks, and wide, dark, yellow-ringed eyes had found a perfect setting. As she gazed at us her eyes were not fierce, indeed she had almost a mild expression. But she was very dignified. People coming down the headland path caused her to leave her perch, and without a sound she slipped away round the cliff. Then we saw that the brooding tiercel was shuffling uneasily and, suddenly, he stood up and flickered away from the nest. Above its edge we saw the tiny white, swaying head and neck of a chick.

Only a few moments elapsed before the falcon appeared at the nest side. She gazed

59

FALCON FEEDING CHICK

intently at the chick, then at us, and finally shuffled over the nest to brood. She was just settling down for what looked like a quiet doze when the tiercel, mobbed by an angry Herring Gull, shot into the cliff and came to rest near the nest side. His blue back was turned towards us, but he twisted his head round to keep an eye on us, and did not move from this position while he rested there. Falcon and tiercel remained there long enough for me to make a rough drawing of them and their environment. Suddenly the tiercel began to call, a long whining note which seemed to be directed at the falcon for she roused and regarded him intently. He left his resting place and glided away, and soon the falcon followed.

The hollow of the nest was fairly deep, but a careful scrutiny revealed only the one tiny chick. A dark shape flashed downwards past the lens of the telescope and, a moment afterwards, the falcon appeared between our cliff and the nesting cliff with something held dangling in her claw. We could not identify her burden, but it certainly was not feathered for, when she alighted at the nest and began to tear at the prey, no feathers floated away. It may have been a vole snatched from a grassy shoulder of the cliff below us. The falcon began to feed the chick, tearing minute fragments from her victim and reaching into the nest to the white swaying head. Sometimes, in her exertions, she slipped half into the nest. Eventually, the chick appearing satisfied, she swallowed the remainder of the prey herself and, with a final look round, settled down to brood. The tiercel did not appear again while we were on the cliff.

JUNE 3RD. For some time past W. and I had conspired to visit Llugwy Bay and to-day fine weather plus a lull in the work while awaiting instructions, and a desire to visit the other side of the island were more than enough to send us there, for it is a place of happy memories. Behind the bay, between fields and shore, there is a narrow area of dunes, and to-day these were decorated with the blooms of the sweetly-scented burnet rose, lovely in their pale cream purity. At Llugwy we expected terns and were not disappointed, for near the sea's edge there was a flock of them resting on the wet sand, in company with Herring Gulls and Blackbacks. Slowly we approached them, a flock of perhaps a hundred and twenty birds, some

Falcon and Tiercel at the Nest

ROSEATE AND COMMON TERNS

appeared dark grey in colour and these puzzled us until we moved closer and saw that they were Common Terns. But what, then, were the pale grey birds, with the black bills and long tail streamers? Surely not Roseate Terns? But that is what they were and there must have been about seventy of them in the flock. We were overwhelmed with such riches, and gazed in delight at these birds which, up to now, we had considered as great rarities. We feasted on their elegant shapes, their pure, pale-grey backs and delicate pink breasts, and could not take our eyes from them. Their breasts, in the sunlight, shone like pale pink satin, and their crowns and crests were of a velvety blackness. Long tail streamers made a perfect finish to a perfect bird. When they rose from or alighted on the sand the whip-like tail streamers bent and waved in time to the beat of the wings. But it was while indulging in display behaviour that the bird was seen to perfection, for then the wings were held away from the body with the elbows thrust forward, and flights crossed behind tail feathers which were erected in a shape like a delicate white tuning fork. Sometimes three birds would display together, (probably two males and a female) and would pace round in a small area, all with wings crossed and tails erect, and making the most wonderful compositions and patterns. Usually these triangular displays ended in a flurry as one male attacked the other. Often a bird would fly from the sea with a sand eel dangling from its bill and, alighting amidst the flock, would walk—nay waddle would be more correct, for this dainty creature does waddle—from bird to bird until he found the female for his favour. He would then present the eel, which she at once swallowed in the most matter of fact manner, while he would pose with head and tail pointing skyward for a moment before taking flight. Sometimes, when a bird landed with a fish, he would not present it at once but would pace to and fro, tantalisingly, a few inches before the bill of the female, which would open to receive the fish only to find it snatched away again.

We stared and enjoyed until our arms ached with continued holding of the field-glasses so, having absorbed as much as I was able of the appearance of the terns, we walked across the beach to the rocks where I made drawings.

It was while we were eating sandwiches, and gazing at the black dots on the pearly sea

ROSEATE TERN

which were Guillemots and Razorbills, that I saw two divers surface not far from the shore. They were Red-throated Divers without a doubt. That slightly *retroussé* look of their bills was sure identification. The puzzling thing was that they were neither grey of neck nor red of throat, but seemed to be still in winter or juvenile plumage, with white throat and foreneck at a time when their kin on the Sutherland lochs would be in full breeding dress.

Clouds had obscured the sun before we left and had cleared the beach of people. We took a last, long look at the Roseates, climbed the dunes, once again admired the burnet roses, and so to the car in the little narrow lane which was haunted by Linnets and Yellow-hammers.

BURNET ROSES

JUNE 5TH. The Stonechats of the gorsey patch by the house have been lucky with their nesting for, on looking through the lounge window this afternoon, I saw both cock and hen preening on the wire fence and, beyond them, flitting about the gorse, at least three striped and spotted youngsters. When the cock approached one of the young it fluttered its wings and asked for food, but he ignored it and resumed his preening.

In the evening I went along the road to the far field pool intent on making drawings of Shoveler. Four drakes were there this evening, feeding and preening; but my attention was diverted by a splashing at the grassy edge of the pond and there the glasses found a Shoveler duck with nine ducklings. Like Mallard ducklings they were lively and foraged about for food, though they were not quite so adventurous, for they did not wander far from their parent. She took them among the grass tufts growing in the water, and then across the more open water, her neck erect and alert, the ducklings following after in single file. The brood must have been several days old at least and, as they swam behind their mother and showed in silhouette against the water, their Shoveler bills, even at this early stage, could be discerned. Presently the family moved to a grassy spit and landed, the duck gathering her ducklings around her preparatory to covering them. She opened her blue-grey wings and, shuffling about, made many attempts before she succeeded in covering all her offspring. Then, for a

62

SHOVELER BROOD

time, all was quiet, but, as she rested on the grass, it was noticeable that the drakes, whenever they approached her, bowed their heads as if saluting her. The climax to this came when three of the drakes came to within six or seven feet of her, one in front, another to the side, and one behind her. There they stopped, half floating, half standing, and all began to bow their heads, a peculiar motion in which the bill was kept parallel to the water, all the movement being made by the neck. Up and down went the three dark green heads, and the duck reacted by opening and closing her bill. She opened it wide but, as the wind was blowing hard, I could not hear if she were calling. Then she, also, began the up and down movement of head and neck, and this went on for a time until she suddenly decided to end the affair, and slid into the water leaving the ducklings in a compact surprised looking group on the grass. They quickly followed her through the grasses and bog-bean, and began to feed again. The three drakes resumed their feeding or preening but the fourth drake remained where he had been sitting, not far from the brooding duck, during the whole of the bowing. Stolid, aloof and still, he had done no bowing and I concluded that he must be the husband and father.

Three Teal were among the bog-bean at the far side of the pool, two drakes and a duck. They went to the bank to preen and a beam of sun made their wet breasts sparkle. Three half-fledged Lapwings walked gawkishly about the pasture beyond the pool, their parents keeping watch by the water. Sentinel parents are very necessary for hawks are observed almost every day and, while I had been watching the Shovelers, I had also caught a glimpse of the Montagu's Harrier quartering the fields away up the marsh.

Shelduck are not nearly so much in evidence on the pools. No pairs are to be seen,

SHOVELER DRAKES POSTURING BEFORE DUCK

63

LAPWING CHICKS

only solitary birds—and these nearly always drakes. Occasionally one catches sight of them flying among the dunes—they, too, must be full of family cares, and this year another anxiety is added, for the dunes are to be turned into forest and, already, large areas are surrounded by rabbit-proof netting. Will the young Shelduck be able to negotiate this obstacle when they are ready to leave the burrows and take to pool and estuary?

JUNE 6TH. To-day has been one of great clouds and grape-blue mountains, with gleams of intermittent sunlight which have revealed the landscape at its best. This evening the air above Cob Lake seemed to be seething with birds; Common Terns, Black-headed Gulls, and many Swifts and Swallows all hunted in their own manner above the water. At the village end of Cob Lake swam a solitary, quiet Pochard duck, and, some yards away from it, a Sheldrake. Abruptly the Sheldrake took wing and attacked the Pochard, which immediately dived. Another Sheldrake, attracted by the splash and disturbance, joined the first. These two could see the Pochard in the shallow water, and as soon as it surfaced they made a joint attack and caused it to dive again, almost hovering over the water to follow the course of the submerged Pochard. It had to surface again, and again the Sheldrakes were upon it. The Pochard lingered no longer but, with a skittering run, rose off the pool with the Sheldrakes on its tail. Putting on a fine burst of speed it managed to outdistance its pursuers which returned to the lake. The Pochard was little worried, it also returned to the pool and this time was left in peace. A Common Tern gave us an exquisite close-up view as it fished by the roadside only twenty feet away. There is wonderful flexing of body as well as of tail when hovering. All day a solitary Whimbrel has haunted the shore, feeding by the riverside and running about the flats among the Gulls and Oystercatchers.

OYSTERCATCHER, WHIMBREL AND BLACK-HEADED GULLS

JUNE 8TH. This evening, while working in the garden, I heard the call of Whimbrel on the estuary and, going to the front of the house, was in time to see two Whimbrel flying above the river. Still calling they circled round over the Cob, over the village and the house and, as they circled, they gained height steadily. As they came directly overhead I imitated their whistle, and saw one bird half pause in its flight and wheel away from the other as if to investigate the sound coming from the ground. It was deceived only for a moment and was soon winging after its companion. They circled once more, still higher and still calling, then, seeming to decide that they had gained sufficient height, they flew directly into the yellow light of the sinking sun, and disappeared beyond the wooded skyline of Bodorgan, their high calls becoming fainter and fainter in the distant north-west sky.

SKYLARK

JUNE 10TH. The song of Skylarks filled the morning sky as I walked along the road by Cob Lake, and a blusterous wind seemed to urge the larks to even greater efforts than usual. Their song was all around and, looking about me, I saw a Skylark standing on a tussocky sod, singing lustily, his crest half-raised, throat throbbing, and body shaking as he poured out his song as melodiously as any of his brethren in the sky. Farther along the road, where stunted gorse bushes grow between road and cob, a cock Reed-bunting perched on a frost-withered spike and made his lowly contribution to the song of the morning, but alas! in spite of his swelling throat, his two little notes, oft repeated, were scarcely audible above the sound of the wind, which rocked his perch and blew his tail so awry that the white outer feathers waved hither and thither. Still he did his little best, and he was a very dapper bird.

JUNE 11TH. I had taken frequent looks at the sunny day from the stuido window and, determined not to miss all of it, W. and I went to Porth Cwyfan in the evening, and walked along the low headland of springy turf on the south side of the bay. Here thrift was growing in beautiful clumps and drifts everywhere; from crannies in the old stone walls, from the turf itself, and from the rocks. Sea milkwort crept among the rocks and stones, small and exquisite, and vernal squill still made a brave show although it was past its prime.

REED-BUNTING

Where the green headland runs down to flat tables of rock we were brought to a halt by a tern rising from the rocks and flying around us in a most suspicious manner. We marked the place from which we thought it had risen and W. was the lucky one, for soon she pointed to the ground at her feet. I went over to her and saw a solitary tern's egg in a shallow crevice of the rock. Grey lichen and a single bloom of sea-pink grew round and by the egg. The tern did not linger above us but disappeared and, as we did not wish to cause her to desert the nest, we walked on. As we climbed to the top of the rocks again and looked across the water at the Rivals we became aware of a great turmoil of birds on the sea, perhaps three-

65

OYSTERCATCHER'S NEST

quarters of a mile out. We lay on the flat rocks and focused glasses which revealed, first, a great collection of Herring Gulls flying, plunging, and floating. Among them could be discerned the sable wings of Great Black-backed Gulls. At the forefront of the disturbance were hundreds of terns—thin flickering grey and white shapes which plunged and plunged. At the rear were rafts of Razorbills and Guillemots, diving continuously. We wished ourselves a thousand yards nearer for there it must have been an amazing sight. I had been watching for some minutes before I discerned other birds shimmering around the milling flock. Sometimes these would show as black shapes, at other times they would flicker white; some plunged among the gulls. They were Manx Shearwaters. The great seething, plunging host moved slowly south-east, in the direction of Llandwyn Island, obviously following a large shoal of fry, and feeding voraciously. We watched for perhaps twenty minutes, and during this time many thousands of small fish must have been devoured.

Then we noticed that the Shearwaters had disappeared from the mob; then gulls began to stream towards us and, soon, were resting in a crowd on a rock islet off-shore, and the terns were making their way towards Llandwyn. Presently the only birds left at the scene of the massacre were Razorbills and Guillemots, and many of these were now preening and tipping over to reveal gleaming white undersides.

We returned the way we had come and again the tern left her nest. A dozen yards away from the tern's nest W. found that of an Oystercatcher. The pair had watched our activities from various rocky points, and now flew off yelping in dismay. The nest-hollow in the rock contained three eggs, and around it were arranged several white winkle shells; this nest also had its spray of sea-pink. We came away as the quietly rising tide was filling the bay round the island of the little stone church.

JUNE 15TH. A morning of cold wind and cloud-filled sky greeted me as I went out at nine o'clock to Cob Lake. There six Herons stood, still and intent, watching the wind-disturbed surface below them. Lower down the water, on the grassy peninsular a flock of Oyster-catchers rested and, with them, Redshanks, Black-headed Gulls and Common Terns, all with

66

their heads to the wind. On the muddy shore near them was a pair of Shelduck. Suddenly every bird was in the air. Herons rose and beat up over the Cob, Oystercatchers winged away in a quick turn which took them over the road and across the Bont Farm fields, to descend by the field pool, gulls and terns circled the lake and Redshanks went to several points of the compass. I looked up at the sky expecting to see the dark silhouette of a Peregrine, but none could I see, though I am convinced that there was one about for all the birds seemed struck by a sudden panic, all that is, except the Shelduck pair which remained unmoved on their patch of muddy shore.

At the far end of the Cob I went on to the saltings and focused glasses on the wet sands where numbers of Shelduck were feeding. Swinging the glasses about I found an isolated pair, and, with them, a brood of fourteen ducklings all feeding on the sand. This is the first brood I have seen this year. Last year, on a visit, we found two broods, of nine and ten, on Cob Lake in late May. None have been brought to the lake this year so far, and it may be that wire-netting of the afforested dunes has diverted the broods elsewhere.

For a time I sheltered in the lee of the Cob and watched the pair of Shelduck on the lake. The drake, like other drakes I have noted recently, was losing the knob at the base of the bill, and its glowing colour seemed to have faded a little. Otherwise he was still a very fine, immaculate bird. Not so his duck, for she was looking definitely frowsy. There was an untidy gap in the feathers of her nape and a patch of pale grey near the bill. Her chestnut band was narrow and dull, and her body feathers generally were much less tidy than those of her mate. I wondered if she were brooding and, if so, where, and would she ultimately bring her ducklings to the lake. When hands were numb through holding glasses I returned home. The black cows which grazed on the lee side of the Cob looked cold in the unseasonable north-east wind.

Later the day improved. Grey skies gave place to Blue and the sun shone. At three o'clock we were at the other side of the island with friends, Wack and Margot, and heading for Dulas Bay by way of narrow, winding, leafy lanes. Dulas is really an estuary whose tidal sands cut inland for a mile. Near the sea a raised tongue of land runs across the mouth of the estuary, this raised bank being broken only by the narrow river channel. On the seaward side of the bank is the sloping beach proper, a beach of sand and shingle, of boulders and slippery green stones, and weed-draped rocks. The raised bank was the objective of our visit for we had heard that terns nested upon it. We walked slowly along, putting an Oystercatcher from her nest and three eggs, but did not find any terns, though the sandy top of the bank with its

SHELDUCK FAMILY

RINGED PLOVER CHICK

growth of marram grass and burnet rose seemed ideal tern ground. As we neared the end of the bank and came to the river a pair of terns circled round us, buoyant and elegant, with slowly beating wings. They called and again the call identified them, for we are beginning to know the harsh note of the Roseate Tern. But there were no nests as yet on y Darran (the Welsh name for the raised bank), so we sat on the seaward side of the bank, had tea, and watched a pair of worried Ringed Plover running about among the stones on the beach. I watched them for a time and then was aware of other tinier forms moving among the stones. They were Ringed Plover chicks and, as I was keen to get drawings of one, I marked where they were and made a dash over the boulder-strewn beach. The old birds called, the chicks disappeared completely among the grey mottled stones, and my search was fruitless. I returned to the top of the bank and resumed my tea. Later I saw the chicks again, nearer the sea this time and in easier terrain of sand and boulders. So I made a second dash and, after a short search, came upon a chick crouching against a grey stone. The chick seemed to be the offspring of the stone itself, mottled grey against mottled grey. I picked it up and it was in no way perturbed, but lay in my hand quietly. I gave it to W. who held it while I made a drawing. It crouched on her palm and did not move. Then as I wanted the underside of the chick W. turned it over and it lay quietly on its back with legs in the air until I had completed another drawing. Right way up again the chick still remained quiet and I was able

RESTING AFTER FEEDING

68

RINGED PLOVER PERFORMER, TURNSTONE SPECTATORS

to make more drawings but noticed that, owing to the heat of the sun on its back and W.'s warm hand below it, it was beginning to pant with its bill held slightly open. So we took it down to the beach where, after several moments of complete stillness in a crouching attitude, it got to its feet and ran with speed among the grey stones and was soon lost to us.

Between Dulas Island and the beach Gannets were fishing and, as they seemed to be hunting fairly close inshore, we went down to the water's edge, sliding over the slippery green weed and boulders till we came to the waves. Here the glasses picked out every detail of the Gannets as they searched, tipped up, and plunged, cream-white, black-tipped arrow heads, whose vanes closed just before hitting the water. Not all were cream-white, for there were immature birds there also, dark and mottled of plumage and one or two very dark. Often the Gannets rested on the water, and at one time all the company, comprising about a dozen birds, was floating on the sea like a flock of geese.

We spent the evening on the rocks beyond Moelfre. Wack was guide and, as we approached the shore, he pointed to a white spot on the low grassy headland above the beach. In the glasses the white spot became a Common Tern sitting on her nest. As we approached she departed leaving three beautiful eggs in their hollow, earthy cup. A blossom of sea-pink was showing in the centre of the nest between the eggs and, when we moved them slightly the flower-stalk was released and the blossom overhung the nest. The three eggs were well matched in colour, but this was not the case in another nest, which Wack showed me, situated on the rocky beach itself. In this case all three eggs were different, both in ground colour and markings. Two of them were heavily blotched, with one or two of their spots as big as sixpences. Also on this beach was a pair of Ring Plover and, as we wandered about the flat-topped rocks, the female behaved in the strangest manner. For a moment she stood with her tail depressed and touching the rock, then, half crouched, she lifted one closed wing above her back, then the other as if she were badly crippled and could not open them to fly. She struggled painfully forward for several inches, but she was a very sick bird, almost expiring in fact; she could not use her wings or trim her tail which drooped low and brushed the

69

Roseate Terns

rocks. She fluttered, a pathetic sight, and was in such desperate straits that seven Turnstones, attracted by her behaviour, flew to her and watched her attentively. They stood in a group near her like an audience of stolid old women in dark shawls and blouses, and white aprons. We were inwardly convulsed with laughter. When the Ringed Plover moved to a fresh stance on the rock the Turnstones followed to continue their stolid regard. The pantomime ended only when the Ringed Plover saw that her efforts to attract us were not effective. Then she became a smart, taut bird again and made an end of her posturing, except to depress her tail occasionally. The Turnstones departed to their weed-covered rock by the water's edge and we, deciding to call it a day, made for Wack's summer hut up in the fields.

JUNE 16TH. To-day a young Cormorant, the first I have seen this season, appeared in the river in front of the studio window. Very brown of back and pale of front it dived and fished peacefully enough until a Black-headed Gull stooped at it. The surprised Cormorant uttered a gruff " Wow! " and swam on the surface. Down came the gull again and " Wow! " said the Cormorant, still swimming on the surface. After suffering several more attacks, each of which brought forth a " Wow! " the Cormorant splashed and skittered over the water and took wing. It was surprising that it did not dive to escape the attentions of the gull, but it seemed as if, in its panic, it had suddenly forgotten how to dive.

JUNE 19TH. I felt that I must make an effort to visit the Peregrines on South Stack cliffs so, after working indoors all morning, I was glad to be, by mid-afternoon, on the flowery edge of the great headland. My pleasure was increased when I focused the glasses on the Peregrine's nest, for there was the falcon, in a good light, feeding two well-grown nestlings from a gory mess held under her talons. She glared across at me for several seconds, then bent her beautiful head and neck and resumed her vigorous pulling, straining against the resistance of her steel-strong legs to tear fragments of flesh from the corpse, which she gave to the young birds. Soon they appeared satisfied, and the falcon, changing her position so that she faced outwards, moved her prey which I now identified as a Puffin. Its orange legs stuck up from the torn body and a few feathers floated on to the growth of sea-pinks at the nest edge which was now untidy and streaked with white. The falcon stood gazing seawards, her own crop full and bulging, then, gripping the remains of the Puffin, she left the nest and sailed down the cliff with the prey dangling from one foot. She disappeared below the edge of the cliff on which I was sitting and I turned my attention to the two nestlings which were

FALCON TEARING PREY

RESTING FALCON

moving aimlessly about the nest hollow. One was considerably larger than the other; both were still covered with grey-white down but the beginnings of feathers could be discerned at the centre breast and the wing edges. Presently one staggered to the edge of the nest, turned its " tail " seawards, and evacuated in a white jet over the edge.

My gaze, wandering over the area of cliff near the nest, discovered the falcon perching quietly on a beautiful clump of sea-pink about seven feet from the nest. I had not seen her return to the cliff. She looked very comfortable, matronly, and dignified as she sat there. Presently her eyes half-closed, but she soon roused, lifted one foot and, with her bill, tried to clear away the blood and feathers which adhered to her toes. She was only partially successful in this and, becoming bored with her efforts and feeling the heat of the sun, which was beating full on her back, she walked awkwardly over the sea-pink and nearer to the cliff face where a jutting rock threw a shadow. Here she settled and was just going off into, what appeared, a quiet doze when the scene was suddenly transformed. The tiercel arrived with something in his claws—it seemed to be a mouse or vole—and laid it, pale underside uppermost, on the brown earthy cushion inside the sea-pink border. This brought such a yelping and a chattering from the falcon, answered just as shrilly by the tiercel, that, for a moment, the calls of the Peregrines competed with those of gulls and guillemots. Then there was a tussle and a flurry of wings and, next moment, the falcon was away with the tiercel's catch dangling in her foot. She carried it away in the same direction as she had taken with the Puffin remains, leaving the tiercel resting on his tail with his legs and feet spread out before him, and with a dazed expression about him as if he were trying to recollect just what had happened to him. He remained in this " spread-eagle " pose for some minutes. Presently the falcon having disposed of the tiercel's capture, returned to a perch on a withered clump of sea-pink near him. The tiercel, now more composed, gathered himself into a more dignified attitude and rested on the flat shelf of earth with his back to his mate. She ignored him and soon had settled herself, fluffing out her flank feathers and bringing up her right foot under them, letting her weight settle on to her left foot. There the tiercel and falcon rested, handsome and beautiful, and, but for occasional quick turns of their heads, did not move again while I watched.

Turning again to the nest I saw that the hot sun was causing the nestlings to pant, their bills slightly open. They moved restlessly about the nest and finally both huddled into a corner where there was a little shade, and slept.

DAZED TIERCEL

JUNE 20TH. I stopped on the road this evening to watch a heron fishing in the shallows of Cob Lake. The lake was very still and so was the heron; his neck outstretched, he stood gazing down, then, like lightning he struck. He seemed to have missed but almost at once struck again, striding forward as he did so. He moved and struck seven times before

TOP OF THE COB

bringing to light his prey—a large eel which writhed and twisted, wrapping itself around the bill, its tail at times beating the heron's forehead and crown. However there was no escape and, stepping carefully through the shallows to the shore, the heron walked with slow deliberate strides up the grassy slope of the Cob until he reached the top and his shape appeared against the sky. Here he dropped the convulsive eel on the grass and stabbed at it. It wriggled about the grass, was promptly hauled back and given another stab. Time after time the eel was stabbed, then the heron picked it up and tried to get it in position for swallowing. But the eel was large and it was several minutes before it disappeared, and even then its tail re-emerged between the mandibles more than once. With distended throat and spasmodic jerks of head and neck the heron gulped and swallowed until finally the battle was won and all that could be seen of the eel was a swelling of the heron's neck. He stood for a moment then opened his great wings and glided down the slope of the Cob, coming to rest in the shallows where he resumed his hunting.

At the far end of the Cob, where it almost abuts on to the road, there arose a great hulla-balloo. Redshanks were yelping and swooping and sometimes perching on the wall to call and pipe hysterically. A poaching cat jumped from behind the wall on to the coping stones and ran along the road followed by no fewer than seven alarmed Redshanks. Their frantic piping had barely subsided when another fracas started in the opposite direction—over the Cob itself and the saltings beyond. This time the cock Montagu's Harrier was the culprit, and he dived, and swooped, and side-slipped to escape the Redshanks, the Lapwings and the Curlew which beset him from above and below and from all sides. The Curlew were parti-cularly vicious, diving on him almost like Peregrines. As he became silhouetted against the sky I saw that the Harrier was carrying something in his foot. The shrieking mob followed him up the marsh and soon all were lost to sight behind the crest of a dune. I, hoping that the Harrier would reappear, went on to the marsh and was, in my turn, mobbed by Redshanks, Lapwings and Curlew. But no Harrier appeared so I sat down and made notes of the flying shapes of my protesting escort.

HARRIER MOBBED

The dunes are full of flowers. Viper's Bugloss stands in spires of blue as vivid as any delphinium; ragged robin blooms in delicate patches of pink, and in the damp places yellow iris is in flower.   Hugging the sand the fluffy seed-heads of creeping willow mingle with heartease of an amazing variety of colours from deep blue through yellow to white.   Among all this the Wheatears, both young and adult, fly round close to the ground, or perch on some dead stalk and utter their " Tcheck! Tcheck! " flashing their pied tails as they take wing.

JUNE 24TH.   On Cob Lake this morning I found a family of Shel-duck swimming there—three ducklings and their parents.   The ducklings were probably over a week old and were very lively, swimming hither and thither, dipping their heads below the sur-face of the water and sometimes trying to up-end.   In this they were not very successful and after a few futile, splashing kicks their buoyant bodies righted themselves. The duck kept a watchful eye on them and swam with them wherever they went, but the drake occupied himself in attacking any other Shelduck which came to the pool and driving them off over the Cob or across the road.   Sometimes these flights soared steeply upwards with a great display of wings and tail, beautiful to see. (It was noticeable that the attacking drake maintained a menacing pose even in flight, for his bristling neck was more arched and down-bent than was that of the pursued.)

ANXIOUS PARENT

73

SHELDUCKLINGS

JUNE 26TH. On a short visit to the lake to-day I discovered the Shelduck family resting among the grass tussocks at the base of the Cob. The parents were with them but, presently, the drake walked sedately up the slope of the Cob and when half-way up stopped and called as if trying to entice the ducklings to climb over the Cob and on to the estuary sands. They, however, preferred to stay in their cosy grassy pocket. The drake climbed to the top of the Cob and again called, but was quite ignored. He floated down in a beautiful glide and landed near the ducklings but soon commenced his solemn walk up the slope once more, calling again, and again getting no response from his ducklings. The duck stayed near the young and fed at the edge of the muddy shore. Suddenly the calls of the drake became a loud throaty staccato as he took wing and landed in the middle of the lake. The ducklings this time heeded his call and skittered from the bank in a rush, followed by their swiftly swimming mother, and soon the whole family were together on the water, the parents alert and regardful of a stout figure with a white dog approaching along the Cob.

JUNE 27TH. At low tide this morning a flock of young Lapwings rested by the bend of the river, and with them were Redshanks, Black-headed Gulls, a Lesser Black-backed Gull, five Oystercatchers and two Curlew. Between the river and the Cob a solitary Whimbrel walked about the shining sand, and on that part of the river nearest to the garden wall a young brown Cormorant rested. Standing on the largest of the little rocks in the river were two Common Terns. While all these birds were in full view of my studio window I could not settle to work but submitted easily to temptation and watched. Then the garden wall itself was suddenly capped by a row of Starlings, both young and old; the young, with their dull brown backs and pale throats, seeming like birds of a different species. The show was not over

RIVERSIDE GATHERING

STARLINGS, NINE JUVENILES AND TWO ADULTS

yet for several families of House Sparrows came to the wall where the young fluttered along the coping up to their parents, with wings open and vibrating, and asked for food to be put into their wide-open and yellow-gaped mouths.

Now is the season of young birds and the garden has been invaded by Sparrow and Starling flocks for some days, while young and old Jackdaws fly about the house in a black squadron of six and perch on the walls and roofs ready for any scraps which W. puts out. The flock of young Lapwings was a reminder that we had passed the period of the longest days, and that soon the time for the trimming of lamps would be upon us.

JUNE 29TH. To y Darran again this afternoon, picking up Wack and Margot on the way. We are convinced that terns nest on the spit which heads the beach and on this our second visit our hopes ran high. Sure enough, when we arrived at the raised ridge, capped by its burnet roses and marram grass, terns were flying overhead. Our party split up, I taking the stony seaward side of the ridge and had not been searching long before I came upon a Ringed Plover's nest with four beautiful eggs laid on a bed of white shell fragments. Cock and hen Ringed Plover loitered or ran on the shingle and were never far away. Farther on I found a tern's nest with two dark-coloured eggs in it; on one the blotches were very large indeed. I made a mark on the beach and continued my search but had no further luck. When we came together again I learned that the others had found an Oystercatcher's and two Common Terns' nests, but we were not satisfied for there were Little Terns overhead, and their nests had not yet been found. We had tea in the lee of the pebble ridge and watched the lovely flight of the terns. Their elegant forms reflected the light from the sunlit shingle and appeared almost incandescent against the blue of the sky. Two of them performed the daintiest of aerial ballets, swooping up together almost vertically, to meet at the top of their swoop and to touch bills. Again and again this flight was repeated and in it there was more of the quality of butterflies than of birds, for wings and tails were spread to the full at the height of the flight. One tern hovered and circled overhead and seemed very uneasy at our presence. Soon it dropped to the shingle, about forty feet away, and shuffled down as if brooding eggs. Here was a nest I had missed. She sat with her head and neck and the wing tips and tail streamers showing above the large pebbles. Any sudden movement by us put her into the air again but she soon returned, making an indescribably beautiful landing. I focussed the glasses on her and, to my surprise, saw that her blood-red bill had no vestige of black on it. When she first flew we had commented on the length of her tail streamers and, as she alighted on the pebbles, the shortness of her legs. The quality of the red of her bill was different from that of the Common Tern's and we had no doubt that she was of the Arctic species. In her " nest " were two eggs of the same large blotched dark tint as in the one I had found. After tea the others left me to draw while they went in search of Little Terns' nests. Presently they returned

ARCTIC TERNS

having found three nests, one of Ringed Plover, the eggs of which were laid on a broken-shell bed similar to the one I had found; the other two undoubtedly of Little Terns though the two clutches varied, one set of eggs having a pale stone-coloured ground, the other a pale grey blue. So we were more than satisfied with our afternoon for we had not expected to find Arctic Terns, as well as Common and Little Terns, nesting on y Darran.

ARCTIC TERN'S NEST

Ringed Plover and Chicks

PEREGRINES' DOMAIN

JUNE 30TH. By early afternoon I was on the South Stack cliffs again, and a quick look through the glasses showed the nestlings squatting in the nest. No parents were present. I was about to set up the telescope when I heard the high " keck! keck! keck! " of a Peregrine and caught a glimpse of a swiftly flying brownish bird passing the lighthouse rock. It circled round, still calling, and as it presented a side view I saw that it was carrying something. Round it came again and then, passing low under my cliff, swooped up and landed on the tip of the nest and began to tear at its burden which proved to be a Puffin.

The eyesses were now on their feet. How they had grown since my last visit! Now their heads touched the rocky overhang above the nest and, as the falcon fed them she did not need to stoop. The larger of the eyesses was the first to be fed; it was also the more advanced in its fledging for, whereas the smaller eyess still bore wide patches of dull white down through which lines of dark feathers showed, the larger had patches of feathers with lines of down remaining at the edges of mantle, scapulars and tail coverts. Both had much down on their thighs, this creating a most amusing front view, especially in the larger eyess which looked as if it were wearing a striped cravat and waistcoat, billowing white pantaloons, and a slate-grey cloak lined with rather moth-eaten ermine.

When the larger eyess was satisfied the smaller one was fed, and while the falcon was thus occupied the large eyess wobbled about the nest and, on one occasion, passed between the cliff wall and the falcon, jostling her and causing her to shoot out a wing to preserve her balance. Both eyesses now satisfied, the falcon, one foot still gripping the remains of her prey, called repeatedly as if summoning the tiercel, but he did not appear. Then for a time all was quiet but, presently, the larger eyess moved to the falcon and nibbled her chest. She eyed her offspring for a few seconds, then tore more fragments from the orange-legged remains

77

CLEANING HER TOES

and again fed her big child until it was satisfied. After another period of rest the falcon rose on her feet and began to call, then turned round, gripped the Puffin remains and flew with it round the cliff. A minute later she was back and made her perch on a clump of thrift near the nest. Here she called again but no tiercel answered. She moved on to the crest of the round thrift cushion and, stooping, wiped her bill first on one side then on the other. She then returned to the edge, perched and continued with her toilet, paying much attention to her feet. She dozed, lifting one foot, which sometimes dropped and rested on the rock, still clenched. The eyesses moved restlessly about the nest and the bigger one, walking awkwardly to the edge, flapped its wings vigorously, sending clouds of down floating about the nest and the immediate surroundings. As it scrambled back the smaller eyess raised itself and nibbled the chest of its big sister (for I think the eyesses were small tiercel and large falcon). She looked down at him curiously then waddled to a corner of the nest and squatted with her head to the rock. The parent bird roused again and began to call. She flew over the sea in a wide arc, calling all the time, then returned to the cliff. Several times she made these short, questing, noisy journeys but no tiercel came and at last she settled on her cushion of thrift and slept with one foot up. I came away wondering what had happened to the tiercel. (On my last visit it appeared that he was rather henpecked.)

FLEDGELING EXERCISING ITS WINGS

SHELDUCK FAMILY ON COB LAKE

JULY

JULY 1ST. Dick, who sometimes comes to help us reclaim this much neglected acre, asked me this morning if I had seen the dead beast on the Cob. " I do not know what it is but I have seen pictures of it. It smells very much." So I at once went out on to the Cob and found there a dead badger in a very advanced state of decay and, as Dick said, " it smells very much! " A neat square of hide had been cut away from its back, so I suspect that Bangor University students had found it some days ago. I am told that there are no badgers in Anglesey so this one must have been carried by the tides from the mainland. I continued along the Cob to the far end of the lake and there saw a pair of Shelduck with nine very young ducklings. This was more like old times and I was glad to see them. The Shelduck pair with the brood of three were also at this end of the lake, and I should think that all is now set for some pretty clashes between the two sets of parents. In the late afternoon I returned to the Cob with the telescope and paper and pencil, intent on making notes on the Shelduck. Both broods were by the edge and, while I watched, the drake of the smaller family, his nape feathers raised like the hair on an angry dog, laid his neck along the water and swam towards the brood of nine and especially towards the drake. Both drakes met. There was a flurry of black-and-white wings and a great splashing, then both birds took to the air and the chase was carried round the lake. Meanwhile the duck of the nine brood had called to the youngsters and they had dived, one and all, away from the danger area. They dived well, like any young Tufted Duck, and came up in the middle of a reed bed where pale yellow-green stems floated on the surface. The two drakes having ended the chase, came down to the water, the one to join its family of three, the other to the reed bed and its nine ducklings. Apart from these little differences they were good models. It was interesting to note that both of the drakes had almost completely lost the scarlet knob which grows at the base of the bill in the breeding season.

79

HUNTING HARRIER

JULY 4TH. On several occasions during the last week the cock Montagu's Harrier has been sighted, once carrying food in his foot which he took in the direction of the marsh. So this evening we determined to see more of him and, if possible, his mate. We walked across the dunes taking pleasure in the gay colour of heartsease, thyme, bird's-foot trefoil, ragwort, and the spikes of viper's bugloss which seem to like their sandy home for they were as tall as delphiniums.

At a place where there is a great expanse of bog and rush, flanked by rough grazing we saw the grey cock Harrier quartering the ground. We dived for cover where some low, wind-swept sallow bushes grow from a raised dyke and, through the screen of twigs, we watched the hunting bird as, with head lowered, he searched absorbedly, gliding, turning, dropping quickly to lift again before touching ground. Suddenly he lifted his wings and dropped into the rushes with legs extended downwards, reappearing a few seconds later with something gripped in his left foot. He flapped up and, coming nearer to us, alighted on a post where, after a quick turn of the head, he commenced to tear at his prey. Soon he was on the wing again, and making height rapidly he called with a high-pitched note repeatedly and soared above the marsh in circles. Then another bird was seen in the sky beating up towards him. We watched intently for we were sure this was the brown female. Quickly she drew near him and just before she reached him she rolled sideways, clutched and caught the prey which at that precise moment dropped from his foot, and, banking round, she glided down to the rushy expanse and was lost in its depths. We tried to mark the spot where she disappeared with the intention of finding the nest; but—what was this? there were still two Harriers in the sky and both were male birds! We watched again. This newcomer was not quite so immaculate in his grey as the first male. When he drew nearer it was seen that he too had prey in his foot and before long he too began to call, and again a brown female was

TEARING HIS PREY

seen to ascend (but not from the place from which the first female came), and took the prey from him with the same sideways roll, though in this case the distance between the two birds was greater and we had time to see the prey dropping from the male to the female. The precision of the "food pass" was marvellous to watch. She came down and alighted in the rushes and we tried to mark this place also, but felt that it was rather a forlorn hope for the marsh is extensive and intersected by gullies and slimy swamp, and I have to confess that on all previous occasions I have come out of it with my shoes full of either water or mud. Some areas of marsh are quite inaccessible and the nearer we approached the nesting area the softer it became underfoot. Eventually we turned back and were glad to be on firm ground once more with the Harrier's nest still undiscovered. Three of the Harriers soared

THE FOOD PASS

against the blue sky in which were trails of wispy clouds, but it was plain that they were too interested in us and our doings to go about their normal business. Round and round they circled with never a wing beat, long tail closed and feet tucked below tails.

As we made our way down the marsh the evening sun bathed the landscape in a rich yellow light; and high in the sky, against the golden wispy clouds, still soared the three Harriers.

JULY 5TH. A framed map of Anglesey hangs on our walls, and for some time we have been intrigued with a certain large blue spot conspicuous in the interior of the island. This evening we decided to find this spot, and so, by devious little lanes, we made our way north-westward. The lanes were full of flowers; red campion lined the bank and great drifts of honeysuckle flowers filled the slow-moving car with their fragrance, for in some places the hedges were composed of honeysuckle only. Meadow-sweet and wild parsley made cream-white borders, and in places where the roadman had not been round with his hook the car brushed the flowery borders on each side. Everywhere there was colour. On the old stone walls and on the roofs of old farms the yellow stonecrop glowed in exquisite patches which rivalled in vividness the orange lichen which was often its neighbour. Sometimes the little lanes were arched over with wind-swept trees and we glided through tunnels of green. At last, we came to a point from which we could view our blue spot of the map—Llyn Llewenan—a large expanse of fresh water with extensive reed-beds at one end. We gazed with some surprise for all about the lake were groups of Black-headed Gulls, these groups consisting of adults and very young birds. At the edges of reed-beds were more of these mixed companies and

Falcon Feeding Young

flying above the reeds was a crowd of noisy adults; the place was full of their cries. At the northern end of the lake the road runs by the waterside and there we brought the telescope into action. There was no doubt that here was a quite large gullery, for some of the youngsters which rested at the margin of the reeds were only just fledged. I focused the telescope on a great smooth rock which was part of the shore, and on which rested a very mixed assembly of birds. There were adult and very young Black-heads, two Cormorants, and several Coots; but for the moment the young gulls claimed our attention. Two young birds squeaked in front of an adult, their shoulders hunched and heads lowered, but for a time they were ignored. They approached nearer to their parent, one nuzzling her crop with its bill, while the other reached up and nibbled its parent's bill. This brought about the desired result for the parent bird seemed to gulp, then regurgitated a mass of something which the young birds eagerly swallowed. Again they asked for food and, again, they were successful, but, on pestering their parent a third time, it left the rock and settled on the water.

INDUCING PARENT TO REGURGITATE

By the bed of reeds and rushes the flowers of persicaria bloomed in great coral-pink drifts which extended across the water and held many birds. The lake, too, was dotted with birds; Coot and Moorhen, gulls and Tufted Duck and Mallard, all were on the shining expanse with their young, but the family we were especially glad to see was one of Great Crested Grebe for in Anglesey this bird is not common. Here they were, the two parents and three young and, as usual, the young either wanting to be fed or carried. While we watched they wished to be carried and two had already succeeded in mounting their mother's back, but the third could not be accommodated, for there was not even standing room. A little later the parent unloaded the other two.

Intermittently crowds of gulls rose from the reeds with great noise and clamour then glided back into cover. There must have been several thousand gulls hidden from sight. At length we dragged ourselves away from the noisy throng and came home to our estuary, and the map on the wall. The large blue spot was now even more intriguing than before.

LLYN LLYWENAN

JULY 6TH. Feeling that, as the eyesses were developing so rapidly, I ought to keep an eye on the Peregrine's nest, W. and I made an early start for South Stack. A strong wind was blowing into the cliff when we arrived but our usual look-out was fairly sheltered. A hurried glance through the glasses revealed the eyesses resting on a shelf of thrift six inches below the nest. Their heads were hidden behind the thrift but it was obvious they were well fledged. Above the cries of the guillemots came the quick call of a Peregrine " Keck! Keck! Keck! " and soon the falcon was seen circling over the water. With a grand swoop she zoomed up the cliff face and came to rest near the nest, still calling. While I was watching the falcon W. saw the tiercel coming in from over the sea whereupon the falcon left her perch and flew up, again calling. The tiercel came to the cliff and alighted. The falcon then disappeared but soon returned carrying prey in her foot. She brought it to the shelf on which the youngsters rested but they were only mildly interested so the falcon took the food away from them and flew off closely followed by the tiercel. So closely did he follow that I thought he was about to take the falcon's prey; but no, she flew away from him, her burden trailing backwards from the speed of her flight. Presently she returned and alighted on a comfortable cushion of thrift where she first regarded her feet for several seconds, then fluffed out her feathers, shook them and preened, stretching her head back and tipping her tail to reach her under tail coverts, in which position it seemed impossible that she could ever again become the dignified bird of her quieter moments. But soon feathers were all in their place once more and she settled down to doze, head sunk into chest, white eyelids closing the dark eyes for a few seconds, but never longer than that.

FALCON BRINGING PREY

From overhead came a deep croak "Quock! Quock!" The falcon gazed upwards and at once took off, circling up to give battle to three Ravens. She came up with them as they were disappearing over the top of the headland behind us and we saw only her first attack which was avoided by the Ravens. Then all the flying birds disappeared over the skyline and soon the falcon returned to her perch.

The eyesses, meanwhile, scrambled up into the nest proper and there indulged in wing flapping and again puffs of down were sent in all directions; only little tufts of white are now left on the bigger eyess, the brown-edged feathers of wings, back and tail coverts, and the dark-tipped buff feathers of chest, breast, and thighs being almost free of down. The smaller eyess had a few more tufts of white about him but there was little difference in the feather development of the two. It seems that the last down to disappear will be that on the crown for both eyesses are still very hoary-headed. They scrambled about their nest, then seeming to prefer the lower position scrambled down to the shelf of thrift, and there squatted with heads to the cliff, pale-tipped tails sticking outwards, and went to sleep.

Thrift bloomed no longer round the nest; only the pale buff faded flower heads remained. A few white campions still flowered near the eyesses but all their immediate surroundings were streaked white in spite of their cleanly habits. All was quiet by the nest when we left, falcon and eyesses dozing, but the wind was increasing in strength and we were not sorry to leave the blusterous cliff edge.

FALCON PREENING

THE EYESSES FULLY FLEDGED

July 8th. A red-letter evening! I had pulled up by Cob Lake to watch the two broods of Shelduck and a heron with an eel when I chanced to look behind at the shore line, which at this spot almost touches the road. Floating on the water was a small bird which I could see only in silhouette, as I was now looking into the sun, and the bird was directly in the dazzling track of the sun's reflection. Was it a young Redshank swimming in the shallows? No, there was something about the shape, a smallness, a delicacy and a poise lacking in a Redshank. The glasses revealed a dark grey head, white throat, a chestnut-brown neck, and a bill with a subtle downward bend at the tip, and then I realised I was looking at my first Red-necked Phalarope. It swam hither and thither, lifted by the wavelets, head dipping quickly and repeatedly to take food from the surface of the water. When not feeding it swam with body high in front, and tail inclined upwards like a little duck. It was quick in all its movements, and when it preened it did so with speed and vigour. Presently it tucked its bill in scapulars and went to sleep. I, wishing to get to the sunward side of it, got out of the car and went on to the grassy part which here juts out into the lake. The bird still slept. I approached with glasses. It roused, then tucked its head round again and dozed. I was now able to see its full colour and, in the bright sunlight, it looked a beautiful little creature. Its pale throat and chestnut neck gleamed and shone, and the two pale buff lines down the back, which seemed to border the mantle, were very distinct. Still nearer, and the white eye ring was now clearly seen, wider above the eye than below. As the fairy-like bird rocked and slept on the water I approached nearer and nearer and eventually managed to get to within fifteen feet. It roused again, stretched its wings straight up above its back, then settled to sleep once more, and I was able to continue with my mental note-making. But I tried the bird too far. When I was twelve feet away it suddenly became taut and took wing, speeding high over the lake on angular wings, with a flight which was somewhat Snipe-like. It passed over the Cob and swept down behind it and was lost to sight. I hurried back to the car, got out a sketch-book and made notes and drawings while the memory was clear. I had been watching the bird over one and a half hours and had not been more than twenty feet away from it at any time.

85

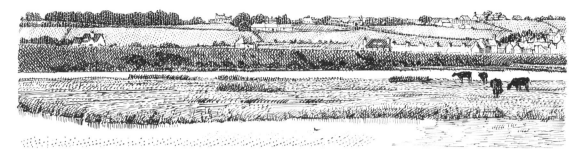

COB LAKE FROM THE ROAD

All the reports of the Phalarope's tameness have been fully corroborated this evening. Comparing my notes with the handbook I think the bird was a female.

JULY 9TH. To the Cob Lake this morning after breakfast on the slender chance that the Phalarope might have returned but she was not there. Instead there was a fine male Black-tailed Godwit, chestnut of head and neck, spangled of scapulars and barred of flanks, feeding vigorously at the village end of the lake.

JULY 10TH. To the lake again, and once more saw a solitary Black-tail, this time a female, and a sick-looking bird. She had a lame left leg or foot, for whenever she attempted to stride forward she almost overbalanced, and it was obvious she was in pain. She fed as best she could, resting most of her weight on her right foot.

JULY 11TH. It was evening when I visited Cob Lake with the intention of making more Shelduck notes. Both broods were at the far end of the lake and near the road, so I quietly pulled up and got to work with the telescope. The ducklings of the nine-brood were on the grass and mud of the shore, feeding away as if for dear life, their dumpy, downy shapes moving hither and thither while their mother swam close by and their father stood by the edge. The three-brood was not far away, and it was evident that the two broods were rather too close for continued harmony. As expected, the drake of the three-brood presently hunched his shoulders, dropped his tail, brought his wings outside his flank feathers and, with

MENACING ATTITUTE OF SHELDRAKE

86

low menacing head, stepped through the shallows and approached the nine ducklings. They went on with their feeding and, to my surprise, the drake turned back and went to his own. Several times this menacing approach was made and nothing happened, but presently the duck of the nine-brood called with a deep, quick " Kack, Kack, Kack," and took the ducklings on to the water. The menacing drake again approached and this time met the father of the nine and at once there was a fine flurry of black and white shapes in which I saw that one drake had gripped the other by the neck. Spray flew in showers as the pair, their wings thrashing, floundered about and for half a minute they were closely locked together. Then one broke away and, with a rush, took wing hotly followed by the other. The chase was taken up the water, then the aggressive drake came back to his duck and three ducklings and after a few spasmodic bows of head and neck settled down. The other drake also returned to his duck looking a little ruffled. In the flurry the nine-brood had moved farther along the grassy peninsula, and when I next saw them they were swimming close to three Black-tailed Godwits, which had arrived unnoticed, and were busy feeding in water which came up to their leg joints; ducklings and Godwits made an extraordinary combination and contrast, the small, rotund, and fluffy against the tall, athletic, and clean-limbed.

SHELDUCKLINGS AND BLACK-TAILED GODWITS

JULY 12TH. By ten o'clock this morning I was climbing the hill to the South Stack again and hoping that I was not too late to see something more of the young Peregrines. The headland was a patchwork of brilliant heather and pale rock and as I walked down the rough track I chanced to look up to the top of the cliff, and there, on the pale rocks, their breasts golden in the morning sun, perched the falcon and one of the eyesses. The falcon began to call and, as I raised the glasses, the eyess took wing and sailed down the rocks and out from the cliff and was lost to view. The falcon also flew, still calling. Reaching my watching place I spied on the nest and saw one eyess sitting there, its back towards me but with its head turned so that it watched me. Beside it was a jumbled shape of feathers and bones and, seeing what seemed to be tail feathers of a young Peregrine in this jumble the thought occurred to me that perhaps this eyess was the young falcon I had seen perching on the rocks above, and the feathers at its feet were all that remained of its young brother. But I soon dismissed this idea for close scrutiny with the telescope showed me that this eyess had not yet attained power of wing, and that it had yet to make its initial flutter from the nest. The falcon came sailing over the water calling hoarsely and soon, with an upward sweep, made her perch on a cushion of thrift. For a time she continued to call, then quietened. Then the tiercel was heard calling over the sea and soon he came into view with something dangling in his foot. He circled round but did not alight at the nest. The falcon watched him from her perch, following his flight with her bright, dark eyes until he swooped to his perch on a clump of flowering hawkbit which grew from the sheer face of the cliff thirty yards from the nest. He could not have chosen a more effective perch wherewith to set off his beauty. There he stayed most of the morning, his white chest gleaming against the cliff. The falcon made several flights returning to different perches near the nest. She is looking a little dowdy and worn, especially about her back which looks brown and ready for a change of coat. On one of her returns she alighted on a cushion of thrift and at once began to clean her bill. I could only surmise what she had been up to, but remembered that several minutes before she landed there had

TIERCEL RESTING

been a great clamouring of gulls farther along the cliffs, in which every gull of the neighbourhood seemed to be in the air.

Happening to look up to the rocks of the headland above the cliff I saw a grey fluttering bird among the patches of rock and heather. It was the eyess falcon. It clambered here and there, moving awkwardly on its pale yellow feet, balancing with a sudden out-thrust of a wing, over bumps and clumps until it reached a flat patch of heather which was a solid mass of bloom. On this patch the eyess stood and opening its wings beat them rapidly for a minute. It was a most beautiful sight. Soon she moved from the patch, wings often being used to help her over the bumpy ground, and finally squatted behind a heather clump over the top of which only her head was visible. At the nest the smaller eyess was up on his feet and tearing away at the remains in the hollow. I could see that some red meat was still on the bones and this he tore greedily, swallowing fragments. When he had fed he scrambled over the edge of the nest and down to the shelf of thrift, where he came to rest with his striped breast facing towards me.

By this time both falcon and tiercel had left the cliff and did not return during the remainder of my stay. Sleeping eyesses, overcast sky, a rising wind and drops of rain induced me to leave the lovely heathery headland after a watch of four hours.

To-day I had been struck by the blue-grey appearance of the eyesses, especially of the young falcon, which appeared much bluer than the adult falcon, while the young tiercel was a dark slate-grey on his back with paler edges to his feathers. Why many bird books insist on the brownness of young Peregrines I do not know.

I called at Cob Lake on my way home and, on the field pool opposite, saw another fine Black-tailed Godwit, so close that I could see every detail of his bars and spots, and glowing chestnut front. These frequent occurrences of Black-tailed Godwits during the summer months are puzzling, for some birds are obviously adult, and one would expect these birds to be on their breeding grounds at this time. Perhaps some day they will nest here! Among the sedges of the field pool young Redshanks fed with a flock of Dunlin and a Snipe. The Dunlin are becoming more numerous as the nesting season draws to a close, and their numbers have increased, during the last fortnight, from a small flock of perhaps a dozen birds to one of over a hundred. Among the black-breasted adults are a few-pale breasted juveniles. Mallard, both young and old, swam and fed on the more open water. All appeared brown birds and if any drakes were in the flock they were in eclipse plumage. The young Redshanks fed on the mud; they were fully fledged, but their flights were still very short and could not be seen beyond

THE MALE EYESS

the wing coverts. Their little tails stuck out conspicuously beyond the wing ends, giving them a gawky, unfinished look; but within a few more days they will be as trim as their parents, one of which flew anxiously about us, sometimes resting on the roadside wall and piping and bobbing uneasily.

JULY 14TH. The South Stack Peregrines are an irresistible attraction. At two-thirty p.m. we were on the cliffs again, scrutinising the rocky buttresses of the face, and the wild garden

EYESS ALIGHTING

89

of the cliff tops, where heather and hawkbit and stonecrop bloomed among the rocks, as colourful as a Persian manuscript. For several minutes no Peregrines were to be seen, and, as expected, the nest was empty, but soon a dark sharp-winged shape was glimpsed as it showed against the blue water and we saw that it was one of the eyesses. The pale tips of its tail feathers were very conspicuous as it opened them to swoop up the cliff. The eyess attempted to alight on a ledge but, misjudging its landing, heeled over and dropped down and out from the cliff to make another swoop up, this time to alight on a little ledge where a patch of heather was in bloom. What perfection of plumage was his! (for it was the male eyess). From cream-tipped tail to dark crown not a feather was out of place. His finely modelled back shone in the sun, and his dark watchful eyes gleamed as he turned his head to regard us.

Out at sea a Peregrine called and the big old falcon came cutting along on stiff wings, almost into the very face of the cliff, but at the last moment she swooped up and made her perch near the nest site. Her cries continued and it seemed as if she were warning the eyess of our presence for he left his perch and flew under our cliff. I moved some yards to the left and, looking over and down, saw the eyess perched on an up-jutting rock, whose lichened shape had for its background the blue water below. The eyess looked perfect in this setting, and rather feverish mental notes were made and some scribbles in the sketch-book. Still another Peregrine came in from the sea, and this time it was the young female which arrived. She is considerably bigger, and of a paler colour generally than her brother, indeed, when she opened her wings in braking to land she looked a pale grey bird against the cliff. At rest she proved to have paler edgings to her feathers, and to have more pale streaks about the crown and forehead than had the small eyess. She alighted on a white-streaked grassy ledge where a few bones and flight feathers lay, and which was obviously the scene of a previous meal. The old falcon called again and the eyess falcon answered with her high falsetto. The eyess was feeling the heat of the afternoon sun for with drooping wings and open bill she panted.

The eyesses flew restlessly from rocky ledge to grassy shelf, sometimes scrambling about the heather and rock of the cliff top, with a queer hopping run as if they were suffering severely from corns. Walking is one of the few actions in which a Peregrine is not dignified. It was

EYESS WING-EXERCISING

EYESSES: MALE ASKING FEMALE FOR FOOD

while they were scrambling thus that the young tiercel exercised his wings. Head to wind, he perched on a flat compact cushion of heather and beat them vigorously for a minute, then stood quite still with wings open as if delighting in the feel of the breeze on them. He stood poised, body held parallel with the ground and wings and tail also held in the same plane. While it lasted it was breath-taking in its beauty. Often the eyesses called, as did the old falcon, which made several flights from her ledge calling all the time. Later she moved into the shadow of an overhanging ledge and settled there.

All was quiet for a time except for the noise of the Guillemot colony, from which came an ever varying discord of noises. Listening to this sound for any length of time one became aware of a sort of underlying melodious chorus, almost like the distant sound of children singing in school, a kind of dreamy background to the more high and discordant noises. Gulls too added their high calls and staccato utterances and, on their own particular rocks, were busy watching or feeding their well-fledged grey young, which looked like fragments of the grey rocks themselves. It was while we were watching the Herring Gulls that we again saw the eyess tiercel flying about the Herring Gulls' own special domain, and, not content with flying round it, he eventually alighted on the rocky crest of it only a few feet away from a pair of young gulls. Down came the old gulls, in swoop after swoop, and at each swoop the tiercel ducked. He endured this for perhaps a minute, then took wing and slipping away from the continued stoops of the gulls, disappeared round a shoulder of cliff. He came into sight again, some moments after, above the cliff top where we now saw the eyess falcon perched on a rock. The young tiercel came down and knocked her off her perch, then swooping up came down on her again, causing her to duck quickly. He repeatedly swooped at her, and at last, she took wing, but in the air she was not free of his attentions for again and again he swooped. She was very adroit in slipping away from him and together they gave a very pretty exhibition of flying. They returned to the cliff top and alighted on a flat rock near the top. At once the young tiercel approached his sister, wings drooped, shoulders hunched, and neck low, and whined as if asking her for food. From her superior height she looked down on him, her big dark eyes regarding him with almost a puzzled look. The next moment

91

he was fondling her chest and nibbling her bill with his; she nibbled his in return, but he got no satisfaction from that and began to whine again. He was obviously hungry. Presently we heard the falcon calling from her retreat down the cliff face and, a moment afterwards, she sailed out from the cliff and swiftly beat out over the water. She turned south and flew down the rocky coast and was soon a black speck in the blue sky with the whole of Lleyn to Bardsey stretched on the horizon below her. She disappeared round the headland of Penrhyn Mawr.

CLIFFS NEAR SOUTH STACK

Perhaps ten minutes elapsed before we heard her calls again and saw her coming in to the cliff with something dangling in her foot. She alighted near the nest, one foot still gripping her prey, and looked up the cliff as if searching for the eyesses. Then she began to pluck the white breast of her prey. Vigorously she worked, her fine head and neck stooped, the inner claws of each foot holding her kill. Soon a mound of white feathers was piled about her and, having exposed the breast of her victim, she began to tear at it in earnest. She fed herself, tearing and swallowing, tearing and swallowing, hungrily. It was impossible to identify the prey with certainty for it was headless. The plumage was black above and white below and the feet were black. It seemed smaller than an adult Razorbill.

Her hunger satisfied she gripped the prey in one foot and took wing, calling as she flew. She swung round and beat up the cliff still calling but failed to see the eyesses which were still together on the rock near the top. Several times the falcon flew round, then went in direct flight to the eyesses and landed with the prey a yard from them. Both eyesses rushed at her, seeming to overwhelm her with beating wings. The prey was knocked into a clump of heather and, in a few moments, the little tiercel emerged from the heather and the hurly-

92

burly with the prey, over which he spread his wings and called whiningly. The old bird stood on the rock a yard away calling continuously, as if admonishing her unruly children. The eyess falcon stood calmly by and watched her brother who presently ceased his whining and began to tear at the carcase. He fed until he was satisfied, then his big sister walked in and without fuss began to tear and swallow. Presently we saw that she was tugging at a leg and soon she had pulled it from the carcase and was attempting to swallow it; she gulped and gulped at the black leg sticking out of her bill. Slowly it disappeared and, as it did so, it made a bulge at the back of the eyess's neck. Slowly the bulge disappeared and the eyess was still for a few moments before resuming her tearing. The little tiercel sat on his tail, crop bulging, wings thrust forward, as if he had fed too well. The old falcon flew away down the cliff and came to rest on a bracket of thrift growing from the sheer cliff face and there went to sleep. When the eyess had finished her meal and was resting beside her brother, both birds very drowsy with food and heat, we came away feeling glad that the Peregrines had been able to rear their young successfully and unmolested.

EYESSES AT PLAY

SHELDUCKLINGS NEARLY FLEDGED

JULY 19TH. This evening to Cob Lake intent on making more notes of the young Shelduck of the three-brood, for they are now half-fledged and in a very interesting state of colour and plumage. Both broods were close together under the Cob when I arrived, but people passing along the Cob drove them towards me as I sat by the roadside, and soon, with the aid of the telescope, I was making all the desired notes of the ducklings. They are strange patchy-looking creatures at the moment; mantles, scapulars, backs and flanks are fledged, as are parts of the heads and necks, and their general colour scheme is one of blacks, whites and greys. The little cheek spot of their extreme youth has developed into an extensive patch which covers the whole cheek behind the eye. The ducklings are no longer pretty.

My note-making was interrupted often to watch the capers of the two drake parents and their frequent chases of each other. There were no serious clashes this evening, indeed these chases seemed to have become almost a ritual for first one drake was the aggressor, then the other, and when either drake returned to his duck he indulged in several jerky bows of head and neck. There was much wing-flapping also in which the drakes sometimes lifted clear of the water. (During these flurries I was able to see the undersides of the drakes and was surprised to note how the chestnut girdle and the black band of the belly had been obscured by many white feathers. The adults are fast developing their eclipse plumage, and this is further noticeable in the heads of the ducks, which are untidy with pale grey patches at the base of the bill). The ducklings of both broods ignored their parents' little differences and fed or slept as the fancy took them, and sometimes their feeding took them almost to the feet of the black cattle standing in the water. Conditions were thundery and the atmosphere heavy— the cows were uneasy, swishing their tails from side to side and, from their behaviour, it was obvious that they were afraid of the attacks of the warble-fly, which always seem to be more active in thundery weather.

Half an hour after the strollers had passed along the Cob the Shelducks returned to its grassy shore, calling their young as they went. The brood of nine followed in a compact little group. The extra thirty yards of increased distance between myself and the ducklings obscured many of the finer details, but as I had fairly complete notes I came away satisfied.

JULY 20TH. What a morning! I awoke to the sound of Curlew and Oystercatchers piping by the river, and on rising and going to the studio window found birds everywhere. On the garden wall was a line of Starlings and sparrows, and beyond, at the bend of the river, there was a fine group of Lapwings, Curlew, Gulls and Oystercatchers. Two herons were flapping lazily from the direction of Bodorgan, over the sands to Cob Lake, their background the blue cloud-capped Rivals. At breakfast the usual sparrow congregation was at the kitchen door awaiting any stray crumbs. W. has made them quite tame, especially one old cock bird

94

SPARROW-HAWK IN THE GARDEN

which always appears whenever we have meals or go outside. This morning I remarked on the jumpiness of the crowd for they would, without any apparent reason, all fly up and hide in a privet bush a few feet away. Presently there was an especially violent panic and with a *brrrrrrr* of wings every sparrow flew to the bush and, an instant later, a barred shape flashed down past the window. W. and I got up from the table and saw a cock Sparrow-hawk standing on the stone wall by the bush. He glared towards the window, then at the bush in which the sparrows were keeping up a constant chatter of alarm. Then the hawk entered the bush, and there was a fluttering of wings and a crescendo of alarm before he emerged on the other side to take his perch on the garden wall once more, where he stood with his barred breast turned towards us. Then one of us must have moved for he took wing suddenly

THE FEMALE EYESS

95

GREENFINCH

and disappeared up the garden. Still there was a quietness about the birds, even the Jackdaws uttered no sound, and I suspected that the hawk had not moved far. Breakfast over I walked up the garden and turned just in time to see his barred shape flash off the tool-shed roof. He flew low by the hedges of the adjacent gardens, then rose, cleared the roofs of the village, and disappeared behind them. With such a start to the day it seemed but natural that mid-morning should find me at the South Stack cliffs again. Reaching a point mid-way down the headland brought me in view of the falcon's cliff. All was quiet. No Peregrines were to be seen or heard. I continued down the slope, almost to the end of the jutting cliff. Eleven feet from the edge I was brought to a sudden halt, for I had caught a glimpse of a barred under-wing and tail disappearing from a shelf just over the edge. I was about to step forward when on this same cliff, which was partly screened by tall grasses, I saw the Eyess Falcon resting. Luckily, when she turned her head I was absolutely still, and she failed to recognise me as something living and turned her head away. I gloated on her beautiful shape and on my amazing luck in finding myself only eleven feet away from a wild falcon. She was a big bird with a fine head. She rested on her breast on the green shelf, her tail projecting and partly lowered over the edge; her wings were relaxed and rested on the turf. I watched for perhaps five minutes, during which I tried to memorise as much as I could. Then something happened; perhaps the oilskin, which I use as a groundsheet, moved in the breeze for she suddenly looked full at me, then literally threw herself from the cliff and swooped away. For a time I watched the two eyesses, and as they flew about the cliff tops and over the water their increased confidence and power of wing was apparent. They glided and swooped, soared and banked, tails now closed as they flew straight, now fully opened in a fan shape as they turned; their flight was beautiful to watch. They disappeared round the far shoulder of cliffs and I saw them no more. But soon after their departure the old falcon arrived, calling loudly as usual, and with something held in her foot. She made her perch on a cliff ledge and, still calling, looked about her, but the eyesses did not reappear. Later she took her prey away from the cliff and, returning without it, alighted on a bracket of sea-pink which jutted from a crack in the vertical rock face. There she rested during the remainder of my stay, her feathers blown out by the breeze, one foot tucked up, her head often stretched sideways to peer out from the cliff as if watching for her wandering children.

JULY 25TH. In mid-June I came to an agreement with a local smallholder that, in return for allowing him to cut and harvest the grass on the acre plot around the house, he would let me have two loads of manure. He has delivered the manure but alas! carting manure is easier than making hay in this chancy July weather. Rain has fallen at frequent intervals, and the grass around the house has grown taller and taller, seed heads have filled, turned yellow and shed their seeds, and the wiry stalks still stand, awaiting the scythe. Among the grasses other

LINNET

Red-Necked Phalarope

plants are now in flower, the white of tall yarrow mingling with the yellow of hawkbit in the wilderness which was once intended for a smooth lawn. Some of the hawkbits have seeded and, this evening, I called W. to the studio window to see a choice collection of birds feeding on the plot in front. A bright and beautiful cock Greenfinch was there in company with a hen and four young birds, a family party no doubt. With them were Linnets, two cocks, a hen and several young. These two cock Linnets, although both were adult, were noticeably different in their plumages, for whereas one, which I assumed to be the older bird, was very grey of flanks and scarlet of chest, the other was buffish on the flanks and pink on the chest. The little birds crept about the stalks, sometimes jumping to reach a high seed-head which, in the case of the hawkbits, was denuded of its seeds by both Linnet and Greenfinch. The

STARLING IN MOULT

Greenfinches were the tidier, cleverer birds in separating the seeds from their down; they would grip the seed-head, pulling off all the seeds with one tug so that stalks were held crosswise in their bills, with seeds sticking out at one side and down at the other. Very adroitly all the seeds would be taken into the bill and stalks and down cut off, so that only the seeds were swallowed, the rest falling to the ground. The Linnets were not so clever for, after they had pulled off the complete head of seeds, they nibbled away letting many seeds fall to the ground in the process, and these they picked up later. It was obvious that the hawkbit seeds were the chief attraction for the Greenfinches and Linnets, but a noisy party of House Sparrows, which suddenly poured down from the roof on to the grass began to grub about and peck busily at the base of the stalks, finding their treasure on or near the ground. From the roof again came another horde, this time of Starlings, which, in a long line, perched on the ridge of the wall-coping, untidy, ragged adults interspersed with neat, brown young. The adults are in moult and look very different from the shining, sleek, iridescent beings they were in the spring. In some the white-tipped winter plumage was showing on the breasts and this feature, together with the unkempt appearance of head and wings turned them into strange,

THRUSH BREAKING SNAIL-SHELLS

outlandish birds. There must have been forty or fifty of them strung out along the wall, when, with a whirr of wings all were away and with them went Sparrows, Linnets and Greenfinches. Along the gravelly drive sauntered the ginger-and-white cat from the nearest cottage.

Of late we have seen more thrushes in the garden than ever before. Some have been young birds, and all have hunted the walls and the rockery for snails which, when found, have been knocked on a stone until the shells have cracked open and the soft body extracted. Scattered about the

97

SHELDUCKLINGS FULLY FLEDGED

garden, wherever there are convenient stones to act as anvils, there are collections of these broken snail shells, and the tap! ta! tap! tap! of a thrush at work can be heard frequently.

More rain threatens. It is several days since we saw the mountains, and this evening a sea mist almost blotted out the far sand-dunes; bad hay-making weather!

JULY 29TH. Early this morning, as I went across the sands for a dip, seven herons lifted lazily from the outer curve of the river bend, and flapped over the Cob to alight somewhere on the lake behind. It was a hazy, dreamy morning. No mountains were visible, and the rising tide made no preceptible movement as it crept into shallow gulley and little creek, turning the narrow river into a wide one, and gradually spreading beyond the river bank and over the flat sands in great shining areas, in which every gull and every Lapwing was faithfully mirrored. A Cormorant, rising clumsily from its fishing in the river channel, shattered the stillness for a few moments, then its black shape sped low over the expanse accompanied by its inverted image, and the ripples died away in the intense calm. As I floated on my back and watched gulls and Lapwings pass over, several formations of Mallard, disturbed by the rattle of a passing milk-lorry, came from Cob Lake and flew over me on their way to the saltings. Since the young have been able to fly there have been Mallard on Cob Lake in the early mornings, but the first buses and milk lorries put them up and they rarely return to the lake during daylight hours.

Later to Cob Lake and found that the parents and family of the three-brooded Shelduck had disappeared from the water, leaving the family of nine and their parents the sole Shelduck population. The nine ducklings are fast following the footsteps of the three in so far as plumage changes are concerned. They have now lost all their downy prettiness and are becoming queer unfinished looking creatures, pied of plumage and gawky of carriage. Out of the water they moved agilely about the mud, bodies held in an upward slope as they ran and, owing to the fact that they had yet but little tail, their legs appeared to be placed too far back. But already they had much of the character and pose of the adults.

At home again I trained the telescope on to the sands of the estuary and searched for Shelduck. Not one could I find, yet a month ago there had been dozens dotted about the flats. The sun shone all day, and in the afternoon above the sands near home, Swallows were flying and some, for a few seconds, rested on the warm sands as if enjoying the heat

98

which was given off. Other Swallows rested on the ridge of the house, and on the slopes of the slate roof, twittering and preening busily. All were young birds with short tail streamers and dull chestnut-buff throats and foreheads, very beautiful in their first plumage. Through the privet bushes and the southernwood young Willow-warblers flitted, bright and immaculate, while at the top of the garden, from under the great leaves of marrow and pumpkin we disturbed four young Blackbirds.

The weather seems to have taken a turn for the better and haymaking is in full swing. All Anglesey smells of hay, hay and meadowsweet and honeysuckle. On this lovely quiet evening it was difficult to imagine raging gales and shrieking winds and, after commenting so, we put thoughts of violent weather from our minds and enjoyed the quiet, and the fragrance, the piping of Oystercatchers and Curlew, and the deep chuckle of a passing Black-backed Gull.

STACKING AT PARC WALL

99

GODWIT QUARREL

AUGUST

AUGUST 2ND. All the Black-tailed Godwits I had so far observed had been peaceful well-behaved birds, with scarcely any sign of bad temper between them, but this evening there were two on Bont Farm pool which were anything but placid. They were feeding well apart, but gradually their concentrated probing of the mud brought them closer and, at once, one bird adopted a menacing attitude, which I had not seen previously. It lowered its head, hunched its shoulders, and raised scapulars and long secondaries until they stood almost on end, and at the same time spread and depressed its tail feathers in the form of a wide and inverted V so that the centre tail feathers made a definite ridge. With peevish calling and open bill, and with slow deliberate steps, it approached the other bird, which in its turn raised its feathers, dropped its tail and faced its aggressor, but suddenly thought better of it and turned away. Later the same thing happened and this time the victim of the attack did not turn away; there was a fine flurry and show of patterned wings and tail, and it was seen that the birds had gripped each other by the bill; thus locked they flew up almost vertically, then broke apart and, after a short chase, resumed their feeding, their raised plumes gradually returning to their normal position. A Snipe, seeming to be infected with the excitement, fluttered from the path of the quarrelling birds and alighted among the tussocks with its tail quite vertical and spread, remaining so for some seconds. Then it, too, resumed its deep probing. Godwit and Snipe made a beautiful trio in a habitat of green grass tufts radiating from pale stems growing from the water and exposed mud.

AUGUST 3RD. It was far too fine to stay indoors, and by afternoon the sunshine became irresistible so that three o'clock found us near Moelfre, and seated on the edge of the low cliffs below the ancient farmhouse, with friend Wack for company. He it was who guided us to a point which commanded a view of the great seaweed-covered rocky tables of the shore

and shared our pleasure in discovering a gathering of terns which rested there. It was an interesting gathering, too, for it consisted of Common and Arctic Terns and two Roseate Terns; and still more interesting was the fact that there was a sprinkling of young birds in the flock. It seemed as if the terns were gathering here in preparation for their southward journey, for Wack told us that similar gatherings had been observed there for some days past.

Some terns were fishing, the adults plunging after their prey as impetuously as ever. On several occasions the juveniles left the rocks and went through all the procedure of fishing, head peering down, sudden braking, and a plunge. Their plunges however, rarely submerged them, and only once did we see one capture a small fish, and this it lost as it rose from the surface. At times, two juveniles were accompanied by an adult, and while the young birds went through the actions of fishing the adult would fly round them holding a fish in its bill as if encouraging them to do likewise. Often the juveniles contented themselves by low dives merely to sip the surface, and on the occasions when they attempted a plunge they appeared to tire quickly and floated on the surface for a few moments to rest and preen. They swam with tails and wing tips held high. It was noticed, too, that when the juveniles rested on the rocks, the adults would fly over the flock with fish dangling from their bills, and often these fish were quite large—large, that is, when compared with the usual size of tern catches. Only once did we see the adults feed a young bird, and it seemed as if these conspicuous and gleaming catches were being used to entice and encourage the young to hunt for themselves.

One of the Roseate Terns rested on a bare patch of rock amid the seaweed, and menaced any other tern which attempted to share the patch. No roseate tinge was noticeable on its breast, and its tail streamers scarce projected beyond the wing tips, but its pale grey back, black bill, and distinctive call were sufficient to identify it. The other Roseate had a white spot where bill joins forehead—the beginning of the white forehead of winter plumage.

Several times, for no apparent reason, the whole flock of about fifty birds rose as one, a whirling exquisite crowd against blue sea and blue sky. On their seaweedy rock they left a busy company of Turnstones. These continued stolidly their search of the weed clumps, quite unmoved by the flighty manœuvres of the terns. There were perhaps a dozen Turnstones in the flock and ten of these were males. It was a bright and beautiful place, this low headland, and the spirit was willing to stay many more hours, but the flesh insisted that it was long past tea-time, and so we made our way past the old grey farmhouse and the field of geese, to Wack's hut where tea and pleasant conversation awaited us.

JUVENILE COMMON TERNS

101

Falcon and Eyesses on the Cliff-top

LAST GLIMPSE

AUGUST 7TH. Visiting relatives' desire to see the South Stack, and a much keener desire on my part to see something further of the falcons were sufficient reasons to send us heading in the direction of Holyhead. The sky was grey with a layer of high cloud which turned the mountains to blue silhouettes sharply outlined. All the way to Holyhead their fine shapes loomed over the Anglesey landscape, of fields and rocks and stone farmhouses, and when we reached South Stack cliffs visibility was so good that we could see the pale blue shape of the Irish Hills on the south-western horizon, and further north the Isle of Man. I searched the cliff face for a possible resting falcon but found none. I swung the glasses on to the cliff of the Guillemots and Razorbills, and though there were enough birds to form a thin chorus of calls, their numbers had greatly diminished, and many of the ledges which had been crowded on July 20th were now quite empty. However the vacating of the ledges by the majority had made it easier to examine individuals, and through the glasses I caught glimpses of young birds which I decided to study more closely later. My niece, who had borrowed the field-glasses a moment before was disgusted at the speed with which I deprived her of them when I caught sight of a dark shape swinging round the cliff below. The shape proved to be

ROUGH DISCIPLINE

the eyess falcon. Now strong and confident of wing she turned and glided and finally came to rest on the great shoulder of rock where many Herring Gulls had nested, and whose grey, well-fledged young were still mewing and nuzzling their parents for food. There she rested on the rocky cornice unmolested by the gulls, during the whole period of our watching. It was while I was watching her that I became aware of a commotion below her. Two Herring Gull parents were belabouring a mewing grey youngster, they pecked and jabbed and chased it from ledge to ledge, and when it tried to take refuge in a cranny it was grabbed by the tail and pulled roughly backwards. At last it was forced to fly, and floundered out from the rock. It was not strong on the wing, and I suspected that its parents were using such rough and forceful methods to compel it to fly.

GUILLEMOT AND YOUNG

To make a closer examination of the Guillemot and Razorbill youngsters I decided to try the steps which twist down the cliffs in a series of hairpin bends and lead eventually to the lighthouse. Half-way down it is possible to see round the corner of the cliff and on to the nesting ledges. As I had hoped there were still a few birds left, and some had young with them. One Guillemot and its chick were particularly well placed for study. Both parent and child were preening when we arrived, and it was interesting to note that the young one stood on its webbed feet like any gull while preening, unlike its parent which rested on the whole of the tarsi in the usual Guillemot fashion. This youngster was partly fledged though its wings were still the merest flippers which it sometimes beat vigorously. I made notes until the chick walked to the parent's side and was taken under her wing, the wing nearest to the cliff face. I had to find another model, and this I did among a group of six Guillemots. My new model, like the first, was preening, but it was much younger and more downy. Its parent was nelping in its toilet, and was engrossed in nibbling and removing down from the infant, especially the down on neck and head. I made notes of this while sitting on a flat seat, which commands a view of the cliff face through a crack in the rock. One of the lighthouse-keepers, at that moment coming up the steps, told me that I was highly honoured, for Queen Victoria had sat on that self-same slab. I could only reply that I hoped she found it more comfortable than did I! Chancing to look along the cliff I saw one of the Peregrines swing into view and approach rapidly. Suddenly it swooped at a Guillemot flying below it. The Guillemot dropped like a stone, " belly landing " with a splash, and dived away. A swift turn, a flicker of wings and a glide took the Peregrine out of sight round the cliff. Almost immediately afterwards a small shape was seen to fall from the cliff, and hurtling after it a Herring Gull. The Herring Gull was swift but not so swift as a Great Black-backed Gull, which reached the water well before its grey-white cousin, and at once jabbed downwards at the small body. After the third jab the Black-back was seen to pick up the body, which I think was that of a young Guillemot, and began to swallow it whole. With backwards jerks of head and neck the Black-back swallowed its prey until only two small webbed feet protruded from the cruel bill. Another gulp, and these also disappeared. The Black-back, its crop bulging, swam to a rocky ledge and rested.

Reverting to the Guillemots we now found that there was scarcely a young one to be seen for all were under the wings of their parents, and, in every case, they were under the wing nearest the cliff face. We climbed back up the twisting staircase, whose treads were too wide for one step, and too narrow for two, and arrived at the top panting and breathless. We leaned on the wall and gazed on the length of Lleyn to the south, with Bardsey like a full stop at the very end of the land, until we had regained breath and our hearts had ceased to pound. The start of our journey home was made to the accompaniment of many hard words from the small niece concerning " that 'orrid Black-back."

In the evening, as the sinking sun glowed below a cloud bank in the west, the mountains were strange and magnificent, strange because of the cloud formation which lay on some of their shoulders like an unrolled fleece. A part of the fleece moved slowly up Snowdon's flank, rolled over his shoulder and his peak, leaving it clear for a few moments.

In the gap between Elio and Snowdon a great cloud, like a pale yellow flame flared up, throwing the rounded contour of Elio into sharp relief. Chasms and precipices of the

EVENING CLOUD, SNOWDON

104

JUVENILE AND ADULT OYSTERCATCHER

mountains were one moment in shadow, the next in bright sunlight, and unfamiliar contours were now revealed in a pageant of form and light indescribable by words. The little farms on the mountainsides gleamed and their windows flashed as they caught the light of the sinking sun. How insignificant the works of man appeared beneath the awe-inspiring magnificence of mountain and cloud!

August 10th. This morning I watched a young Oystercatcher attempting to coax food from its parent. Both birds were on the sand in front of the house and I enjoyed a " grand-stand " view of the performance. The juvenile squeaked and whined by its parent's side and followed every move. When the old bird stood still the young one crouched and passed below its chest, repeating this manœuvre from one side to the other, and later, circling it completely, passed under the breast and tail of the parent, causing it to stand almost on tiptoe. Whenever the adult probed in the sand and found food the juvenile made a little rush to the same place; this indication of the whereabouts of food being all the help it received, it later decided to hunt for itself.

It is a common sight these days to see an adult Herring Gull fly over the house or garden with a brown, squeaking juvenile following closely, and on the beaches these big brown youngsters are often to be seen, hunched before their parents, whining and wheedling in an attempt to induce them to disgorge.

Recently Swifts have been noted in increasing numbers and, for the last few days, we have calculated that there must have been between two and three hundred birds in the air above the Cob Lake. Usually these gatherings have been silent, and there has been none of

SWIFTS

105

that high, excited calling which one hears when a few are playing about high chimneys or church towers. It is plain that the lake is a gathering place for the flocks and that soon they will be away.

On this evening of the tenth they were again cutting the air above the lake but their numbers had diminished noticeably. What tireless fliers they are! with no thought of resting to husband their strength for their long journey—true creatures of the air. Compared with them the Swallows and Sand-martins which were using the lower air seemed weak, fluttering things.

HOT DAY ON THE COB

AUGUST 11TH. All the weather signs seemed to indicate " Set Fair " this fine morning. When I went out to the river for a dip the mountains were only faintly visible through the sunlit haze. By the widening river Herons, Gulls, and Cormorants rested. No bird called and all was quiet over the vast expanse of the estuary. Away out at the bar, three miles distant, there was already a shimmer of heat, and birds on the far sand-bank seemed to be resting in mid-air. By mid-morning the heat had increased so much that I was glad enough to work indoors. From the upper windows I could see the black cattle standing in the shallow and diminishing water of Cob Lake and the field pools, and, among them, a flicker of small birds which proved to be young Pied Wagtails and Starlings feeding on the soft mud. The Swifts have moved on, and after a careful search with the glasses only two were discovered flying about the lake. Not for several years have the island farmers been granted such weather for the hay harvest and, on the high ground on both sides of the marsh, the cleared fields show palely in the chequer-board pattern of pastures and rough land.

This is the time of holiday visitors and, to-day, they were making the most of the weather. Scattered along the grassy length of the Cob little groups of visitors lazed in the warm sun, or ventured across the sands and into the shallows of the river intent on bathing. To-day there were few shrieks as the bathers entered the water for it, too, was warm. Figures dotted the sands here and there wherever the ebbing tide had left any part uncovered, but in spite of that Oystercatchers, Gulls and Cormorants still found lonely spots on which to rest or feed. During the afternoon a vandal visitor ran his car on to the Cob and along it for some seventy yards, before making contact with his acquaintances already on the Cob. We were all up in arms at this desecration and were conspiring to deal drastically with the offender when, to our great joy, the Watcher was seen to stroll along to the car, take its number and then ask for its removal. After a little talk the blot was erased from the landscape.

When the tide was at its lowest and the rocks in the river were fully exposed, a stout figure was seen walking in midstream, prodding here and there with a five-pronged, long-handled fork. In his slow progress along the river he disturbed a small flock of waders. which twisted and turned, twisted and turned about the riverside before alighting again. They were Dunlin, a mixed flock of black-bellied adults and brown, pale-breasted juveniles. Slowly the man worked his way round the bend and to the rocks, and here the bed of the river came in for special attention and much prodding. When he came nearer we could see that there was a string trailing from his waist, and at the end of the string, in the water, was a flat-fish. This he had spiked lower down the river, but he had no luck while we watched. The " fork fisherman," as the young nephew called him, left the river and walked to the grassy shore where he changed his wet, old trousers for dry ones. As he left the beach we tried to do a deal with him over the garden wall, asking him if he would sell that single flat-fish. He thanked us but, saying that he " wanted it for the family," stumped away to the road, the fish dangling in his left hand, the fork in his right.

As evening drew on the Cob and the sands quietened, the visitors went home and the noisy children were put to bed. For the villagers and some visitors the road bridge over the river was now the focal point, and men and youths, girls and boys lined the two parapets and, gazing either up or down stream, discussed this, that, and other things in a regular village parliament. At dusk the sands were quite deserted and I appeared to be the only human on them. In the gathering darkness a great congregation of gulls by the bend of the river gleamed whitely. Over them the sable silhouette of a heron flapped on its way to the tall Bodorgan trees and called querulously. As he went on his way, and was almost lost in

THE "FORK FISHERMAN"

TO-MORROW IS AUGUST THE TWELFTH

the dusk, a formation of five Mallards passed over him and, flying directly over my head was soon lost to sight. Then another formation quickly followed, and still another, and their flighting suddenly reminded me that to-morrow was August 12th, and also brought to mind the men I had seen going to the village inn with guns under their arms. Only a few more hours respite for Ducks and Curlew and the like. Suddenly Bang! Bang! came from the direction of Cob Lake. So some impatient " sportsman " had been unable to wait the remaining few hours, and I suspect that if a visiting shooter is the culprit there will be some hard words uttered in the village pubs. Before the shots the wide expanse was full of bird calls, the cries of Gull and Curlew mingling with the mewing of Lapwing. The shots caused a sudden silence, then a fresh outburst of calls in which was a note of alarm, especially from the Curlew and a much startled Heron which seemed unable to forget the rude shock it had received and complained loudly all the way down the estuary.

I continued across the sands until I reached the fallen masonry of an old mine shaft. Here, resting on a shingle spit and silhouetted against the water, was a large flock of Lapwing. The flock was full of quiet mewings, a lovely sound in the greater quietness. I walked slowly past them and they were not alarmed, but the moment I stopped they rose with a throbbing noise of wings and I was surprised at their numbers, and also pleased, for one is constantly reading reports of the diminution in the Lapwing population of many districts. I turned for home and before I reached the shore wall and the little gate I heard two more shots from the marsh. After midnight we were wakened by more shots and later, as day was breaking, there was a regular fusillade from the marsh and the Cob. So, for a time, it is good-bye to peaceful bird study. Now it will be a case of catch-as-catch-can, during the periods when the gun-men are not about.

AUGUST 13TH. The fine weather continues and, for the last few days, the sun has shone from dawn to dusk with hardly a cloud in the sky. Often it has been unbearably hot and this morning, as I took the car to Cob Lake in preparation for some further study of the young Shelduck, the heat was already appreciable in spite of the early hour. The brood now numbers

Black-Tailed Godwits Fighting

eight, some mishap having befallen the ninth duckling for its corpse lay in the shallows, flat and bedraggled. The eight with their mother were walking to a raised grassy platform when I arrived, and on this foot-high table, above the mud, they all preened vigorously. Their parent was hardly distinguishable from them for she was in " eclipse " and the grey-white patches on her fore-face bore a close resemblance to the faces of the young. She was very dowdy. Gone was the metallic green sheen of head and neck, and the beautiful chestnut girdle and black belly-band of her spring plumage. Even the colour of her bill and legs seemed to have become duller. I made drawings of them as necks turned and twisted to preen half-grown primaries and sepia pale-edged scapulars—the morning sun revealing the fine modelling of their chests and breasts. For half an hour I made notes, then the first of the holidaying visitors came along the Cob and moved the ducklings from their grassy platform, and out on to the mud across which they walked, in a compact group of eight, leggy, pale shapes, until they reached the water. They slipped in among green weed and floating algæ and, in single file, swam to the centre of the water, providing a good opportunity to make notes of swimming poses. By now the sun was blazing down and the car felt like a greenhouse; hands were moist with perspiration which did not benefit the pages of the sketch-book, and eventually I was glad to take refuge in the cool of the house.

Adult ♀
in eclipse

JUVENILE SHELDUCKS

AUGUST 15TH. While having tea W. and I were conscious of the excited calls of gulls and later, on going to the door, we beheld a great gathering of Black-headed Gulls wheeling and soaring above the garden. At first we were at a loss to know why the gulls had chosen to grace our premises with their manœuvres, but soon it was obvious that they were hunting. With short excited cries they interrupted their glides to dart to one side or the other, or sometimes to shoot upwards at a sharp angle. Then we remembered that this was the time

109

when ants were on the wing, and that the garden and the neighbourhood was swarming with them (for I had been well and truly bitten by them while sun-bathing). So the gulls had come to the feast in their scores, nay hundreds, for at one time there must have been several hundred birds circling about. It was a beautiful sight! The bright, afternoon sun turned the wheeling, darting birds into dazzling pale gold shapes against the deep blue of the sky and the shimmering landscape below. We watched for perhaps fifteen minutes, then a few gulls began to drift away riverwards, and soon all had gone from the scene of the feast, and the air above the garden was left to the Swallows, Linnets and Greenfinches again. I went to the front of the house and, from the studio window, looked across to the Cob. Beyond it, above the grey roof of the little farm known as Pen Cob another swishing crowd of gulls was concentrated on another feast of ants. At a distance they looked like a veritable snowstorm above the squat little chimneys of the croft. Soon this second feast was over and the crowd dispersed.

Later in the evening we went along the road which runs up the marsh. On a rough patch of ground covered with heather clumps and scattered gorse bushes a large flock of Common Gulls was seen in company with Rooks, Jackdaws and a few Carrion-crows. The birds were well distributed over the whole of the waste land and I think that they, too, were feeding on ants. I saw my first flock of Common Gulls a week ago and now they are here in strength, but are more often seen on the pastures in company with sheep than on the estuary.

FEAST OF ANTS

AUGUST 18TH. When I went along the road to Cob Lake this evening I found unusual activity in one of the flat fields bordering the road. A crowd of men, boys and girls had gathered there, and with them were greyhounds, the latter being the obvious reason for the motley assembly.

Presently three youths, each with greyhound on leash, walked to the corner of the field nearest to me, where there was a large wooden box containing four stalls, each just large enough for a greyhound. The hinged back was lowered and the three greyhounds were pushed into the box when the back was raised and fastened. Lying on the ground, some fifteen feet from the box, was a stuffed rabbit skin. At a signal a youth jumped on top of the box, waved his arms to a group of men in the opposite corner and, at the same moment, the rabbit skin came to life and leapt miraculously away across the field. Simultaneously the youth pressed down a wooden lever which lifted the front of the box and so released the

TRIAL RUN

dogs. Only two left the trap and, at their greatest speed chased the leaping rabbit skin to the far corner of the field, where they were captured and put on leash again. Here was fixed the contraption which animated the rabbit skin—an old bicycle frame turned upside down and holding one tyre-less wheel in the front forks. Attached to this wheel was a crank handle, and wound round the concave rim was a length of cord to which the rabbit skin was fastened by the neck. A boy took the rabbit skin and ran with it towards the release box, the cord unwinding from the bicycle wheel as he ran across the field.

THE CORD SNAPS

111

Alas for the third greyhound which never left the box! the excitement had proved too much for it and it had fallen into a fit. It was pulled out, a rigid, slavering, brown shape. It lay for some moments, stiff limbs twitching, then began to struggle to its feet, staggering and wild-eyed. It knew no one and seemed filled with fear, for it snapped at anything which approached its muzzle. Its youthful owner covered it with a dark overcoat but this was unavailing and the beast continued to snap and growl. Gradually it returned to normal and recognised its owner who lead it away still weak and shaky.

The next set of dogs to be put into the trap consisted of a tall tawny one, a black one, and, at the last moment, a collie which was popped in by one of the village kids. The front was opened, the rabbit leapt away with all three dogs hot on its tail and the man at the winding gear turned the handle for dear life. The collie did well and was not outstripped by so many yards, but their course ended with the rabbit coming to a dead stop (as the cord snapped) and the two greyhounds turning somersaults over the top of it and all landing in a heap. And so it went on, the last course being run by four of the village kids who put themselves in the box and, as the front went up, shot out on all fours but collapsed in hilarious heaps after a few yards of lolloping.

Whatever the entertainment provided by the forthcoming coursing match I am sure it will be no more varied than was that of the " trials " on this beautiful evening with the bright sunlight illuminating the green meadow, the sleek greyhounds, the bright frocks of the girls and the dark dress of the men, all backed by the distant ridge of Llangaffo with its chequer-board of little fields, and beyond the lilac-blue mountains sharp and distinct against the blue sky.

AUGUST 22ND. This afternoon we, that is " Holly " and Mrs. Holly (who are on a visit to us), Winifred and I, went to the South Stack as I wanted H. to see the Peregrines if possible. When we arrived on the cliffs a strange quietness pervaded everything; even the gulls were quiet. I looked towards the cliffs on which the Guillemots, Razorbills and Puffins had nested. All the ledges were bare, and the cliff-nesters, young and old, had departed, and with them

GREY SEALS

SHELDUCK FLOCK

had gone the chorus of sounds which had echoed about the cliffs all spring and summer. I scrutinised the ledges and the pinnacles for my Peregrines but could not find them and the thought occurred to me that the departure of Guillemots, Razorbills and Puffins meant that the chief food supply of the Peregrines had also disappeared so that now the falcons had no reason to linger in the vicinity. We saw no sign of them during our visit and we had to content ourselves with the solitary Shag which was standing by its well-grown young on the nest at the base of the cliff, and with the Herring Gulls still being pestered for food by their importunate grey youngsters which for their persistence received many a peck and buffet from their parents.

We wandered along the cliff path towards Pen Las rock disturbing a great variety of butterflies on our way. Two Grayling butterflies, resting on the path, brought us to a standstill for they were behaving almost like birds, the one quite still, the other walking round it and opening and closing its wings as it did so, the whole procedure reminding us of the courting display of some birds. At a magnificent part of the cliffs we sat on the smooth heather cushions and had tea. We had reached the jam-sandwich stage when, chancing to look down at the water, I spied a round black object gleaming with a shining high-light. Glasses revealed it to be the head of a seal, and revealed also the seal's mottled body as the animal floated upright in the water. As we watched it pointed its Roman nose heavenward, then lowered it parallel to the water surface and appeared to be directing its misty gaze upwards to us. Soon, with a fat, lazy roll, it submerged and I lost its mottled length in the deep water. It reappeared several times. We were recounting to our friends the weird cries and groans which we had heard the Grey Seal make when, from below, came a soft, hollow, moaning sound. Down among the sunlit wavelets there were now two seals, one much smaller than the other, and this was seen to swim against the larger seal, and rub against its chest and throat. Then they faced each other and, with muzzles almost touching, they gave vent to that hollow moaning sound we had first heard. The big seal disappeared and we saw it no more but the smaller one cruised about and occasionally surfaced. Twice it completely " looped the loop " and presented its pale undersides to us as it swam on its back near the surface.

113

Shag and Nestlings

But that which especially delighted Holly was the colour on the cliff tops, for the heather was still out and among the heather glowed the yellow of the dwarf gorse. Great areas of this lovely patchwork of heather and gorse were in bloom together, broken only by the outcrops of pale-grey rock, the ruggedness and boldness of which did but serve to enhance the delicacy of the flowers. Through this enchanting rock garden we slowly retraced our steps, reluctant to leave the place.

In the evening, as Holly and I leaned on the garden wall, and looked over the sands and the river, a flock of nine Shelduck came swiftly from the direction of the marsh and, beating over the Cob, began a long glide down, alighting eventually on the sands. The flock consisted of eight young and one adult and I suspect that they were the brood which, as ducklings, made the Cob Lake so interesting.

RED ADMIRAL BUTTERFLY

AUGUST 23RD. What a place for butterflies and moths this is! The dry, sunny weather seems favourable to them and the garden is, at present, swarming with them. There are too many Large Whites about for the health of cabbages and sprouts, and there are too many little patches of pale yellow eggs under the leaves. Still the Large Whites are beautiful but I think my real favourite is the Red Admiral, for his colour scheme of black, white and red is bold and definite, yet restrained and choice. This morning Holly captured a Clouded Yellow in the garden, and it seems from all accounts that it is a good year for them. Common Blues flit about the plot of coarse growth, which we hope will eventually become an orchard, and look exquisite when they alight on the yellow ragwort flowers; here too the Cinnabar moth is common, and we bless its striped caterpillars for the good they do in devouring the showy but pestiferous ragwort. Peacock butterflies and Small Tortoiseshells have been with us for some weeks, and have daily graced the privet flowers and a bush of pink rambler roses. Some of the Tortoiseshells have entered the house and have made their way to high dark corners about the landings, resting there as if intent on hibernation. But for behaviour I think the Humming-bird Hawk-moth has proved most interesting. It has occurred several times within the last few days and, this morning, Holly was able to photograph it as it hovered in front of the flowers of the pale-pink soapwort, a bank of which grows just over the garden wall. As it hovered its wings moved so rapidly that all one could see of them was a blur of orange, and as it visited each flower-head its long proboscis was uncurled and thrust among the petals in search of nectar. In flight it was very swift and direct, and shot away at amazing speed as soon as it had finished its search of the soapwort.

HUMMING-BIRD HAWK-MOTH

During the evening we visited the Cromlech called Ty Newydd. A stile over the

114

TY NEWYDD

roadside hedge gave access to a field path between a high banked hedge and a sea of waving, golden-yellow barley. In one corner were the ancient stones consisting of several uprights (in this case reinforced by the addition of brick supports) capped by the great stone roof—a massive boulder lichened and weather-worn. When Holly had taken photographs we examined the stones more closely and found that the warm, sunlit western side of the roof stone was dotted about with Wall Butterflies basking in the last warmth of the day. On the warm stone there were also groups of flies, large and glossy-black of body, with beautiful gold marks on their heads. None of us knew their names, but they were very handsome. Our shadows falling on the stone put butterflies and flies to wing. The great boulder was velvety-smooth to the touch and, being warm, felt almost alive. As we returned along the path we speculated on why and by whom it had been called Ty Newydd—" The New House."

WALL BUTTERFLIES AND UNIDENTIFIED FLIES

115

AUGUST 24TH. As we passed through Aberfraw village this evening there was a savoury smell of fish cooking, fresh fish too, and when we reached the top of the village we met a boy carrying a load of mackerel, each fish threaded by the gills on a string.

At Porth Cwyfan we noticed several groups of men and boys all making for the rocky shore to the south of the bay, and most of them were carrying fishing tackle. I followed them along the close-cropped headland for perhaps half a mile, and then came suddenly upon the place they were heading for—a long spit of rock perhaps thirty yards in length jutting out from the shore. On its seawards side was a motley gathering of men and boys, most of whom were fishing with the strangest assortment of rods imaginable, from whippy elegant fly-rods to bamboo curtain-poles. Lines were baited with silvery white-bait, and at frequent intervals a quivering mackerel was hauled out, unhooked, and thrown on the rocks behind the fishermen. White-bait was netted in an inlet between the spit and the main shore, and, judging by the frequent journeys of the fishermen to the spot, the supply of bait seemed to be unfailing.

The line of fishers (accompanied by the usual greyhounds and lurchers), on the crest of the great rock, their fishing-rods and poles waving, the surge of the rising tide, an occasional gull dipping to the surface to capture some small fry, all this made a most animated scene, enhanced by the background of waves, stretching away and away to where the lighthouse of Llandwyn gleamed golden-white in the evening sunlight, and beyond that to the foot of the mountains whose high tops were in cloud. Out at sea there were other fishers, for Gannets were plunging and sending up spurts of foam as their arrow-head shapes pierced the waves. We could not resist the gleaming mackerel and bought twelve for a shilling, and came away with them dangling on a string.

MACKEREL FISHING

116

COLT BREAKING

AUGUST 25TH. When Holly returned from his pre-breakfast walk he presented me with a dead young Shelduck. It seems that he had met a visiting shooter, an elderly and experienced sportsman, who admitted that he was not sure of the species at which he was shooting, but rather than let the doubtful bird go he shot it, and not only it but a second young Shelduck which was " lost on the sands." (Let no one tell me that the so-called " sportsman " with a gun is usually a good naturalist, I have not found it so.) I decided to make the best of a bad job by making careful plumage drawings of the dead bird, which unfortunately for my purpose, had further suffered by having its head stamped upon by the " sportsman."

The hot weather continues and the trees are looking parched; in some the foliage is as brown as in late autumn. The pastures are baked and arid and the farmers are complaining of the consequent lowering of the milk yield. One farmer this morning brought a colt to the sands because his pastures were too hard for colt breaking. The colt was driven on a long rein and made to trot round in circles, and as the farmer stood by the river edge half the circle was made on the sand and half in the river, all very beneficial to the colt's legs and feet. The whip was used very judicially and the colt was kept at a slow trot except when it decided that it did not like the game. Then there was a bit of pulling and half-rearing, and during one of these bouts it managed to break free and went cantering up the beach towards the road. However, the usual onlookers were, for once, useful, and stopped the colt before it reached the road. It received a few smart strokes of the whip for its lapse then was brought back to its circling in and out of the river again. It seems that all this exercising is in preparation for the Horse Show at Llangefni in early September.

Most of the corn is cut and is so dry that it hardly needs to be left in stook but is fit to stack at once. The field pools by the roadside are dark weedy expanses of mud, and even on Cob Lake the water is much reduced in area and great stretches of mud show in unusual places. There were six Ruffs on the lake this afternoon, elegant, quick-moving birds. Autumn will soon be upon us.

117

AUGUST 27TH.   At seven o'clock this evening the incoming tide had covered the little rocks in the river, indicating that the water was deep enough for a swim, and this, together with the warm sun was all that was needed to induce me to don bathing shorts and away to the bend of the river.   Approaching the bend I saw that I was not to bathe alone for on the other side of the river were scores of spectators all lined up by the water's edge, a delightful crowd consisting of Dunlin and Ringed Plover.   They did not heed my first steps and splashes and ignored me when I was well in with only my head above water.   I swam about for a while in the deep centre channel and watched them, a most interesting experience as the viewpoint was so low.   I approached their side of the river and still they did not move.   Reaching the shallows I put my hands down on the sand and slowly pulled myself still nearer to the birds. At last I was lying on my stomach in only six inches of water and gazing at the nearest bird which was only twelve feet away.   Those nearest moved a few steps up the sand then renewed their preening or sleeping.   This was bird watching de luxe—warm sun on my back, warm water and sand beneath me, no worry of clothing or field-glasses, and the lovely company of birds so close that every detail could be plainly seen.   There were young and old of both species in the flock, the old Dunlin still retaining the black waistcoat of the breeding plumage, while the young were very white on their undersides and their heads and necks had a suffusion of brown which was absent in the adults.   The young Ringed Plover were exquisite and delicate in their colour and pattern and were easily distinguishable from the boldly marked adults.   I drew a little closer.   Heaven knows what the birds thought I was, but W. who was watching from the house, said I looked like a large pink seal.   I raised myself on to my knees; still the birds did not move, but when I got to my feet the whole flock exploded into the air with a great flashing of pale underwings and much shrill whistling.   I swam back across the widening river and while I was rubbing myself down the flock flew past and wheeled about the sand, hither and thither, and finally settled again at a point where three herons stood sleeping in the drowsy evening sunlight.

DUNLIN AND RINGED PLOVER

AUGUST 28TH.   The road from the village into the marsh runs parallel to the high bank of the river for almost three miles before crossing it by a stone bridge.   Between river and road is a canal and, this evening, as we were cruising leisurely along the road W. asked me to stop as she had seen small dark birds swimming under the bank of the channel.   I pulled up just in time to see several Moorhen chicks disappear behind a row of rough vertical timbers which

SIDE CANAL AND RIVER EMBANKMENT

shored up the bank. Suddenly the parent Moorhen created a great hullabaloo and swam
swiftly towards the timbers just as the sinuous, brown shape of a stoat came from behind
them and grabbed one of the chicks. The stoat was in the act of dragging the chick into
a dark cranny when the parent Moorhen charged it, with all feathers on end. The stoat
dropped the chick, which at once dived, and took refuge behind the timbers while the outraged
Moorhen swam back and forth calling loudly, head still lowered menacingly. The stoat, by
devious holes and passages behind timber and herbage retreated along the bank, and we
had only momentary glimpses of it. The Moorhen quite failed to follow the stoat's way of
retreat and still clucked and fussed, feathers on end, at the scene of the disturbance. Gradually
she regained her composure, and calling her four chicks swam with them up the canal, her white
tail coverts flicking and conspicuous in the dark shadow of the bank. Soon the family turned
into a drain which empties itself into the canal and was lost beneath the overhanging grasses.

GREENSHANKS AND REDSHANKS

SEPTEMBER

SEPTEMBER 1ST. This morning was the first for weeks on which a cloudy sky had obscured the rising sun, and on which the mountains showed as something more than the palest of pale ghosts. At 7.30 the river was at its lowest, so low that little rocks not normally visible showed above the surface in the bend of the channel, and there as usual were birds. Lapwings were mewing and squeaking querulously among themselves, and peevishly rushing at other birds, sometimes of their own kind, often at Redshanks of which there were a goodly number. Scattered among them were little groups of Dunlin and Ringed Plover, but the reason for prolonged observation was the presence of two Greenshanks. The Redshank is an elegant bird but seen beside the Greenshank it looks rather dumpy and unfinished. The Greenshanks were feeding in the shallows, with quick vigorous movements in contrast with the more leisurely movements of the Redshank and, again by contrast with the more ponderous dignity of a Curlew, which had captured a small crab and was having difficulty in swallowing it. There was a rush of wings and another flock of birds made as if to alight but suddenly changed direction and sped away down the river. They wheeled back again, came over the flock below when several almost touched ground, but again they changed their minds and again wheeled round. Twice more they made as if to land, then, with a flickering of silvery wings, they alighted among the Lapwings and Redshanks, a lovely congregation of Golden Plover. They stayed by the river until the tide began to flow and cover the little rocks; then, becoming restive, they stretched their wings and flew off in a body over the Cob and away

120

up the marsh. As the water rose Redshank, Dunlin and, last of all, the Lapwings left the riverside. An hour later, when I went in for my dip, Dunlin and Ringed Plover were scattered about the still uncovered sands in large numbers, especially in those areas where there were worm castings. The birds were most difficult to see in the pitted, uneven surface but wherever one looked there were small birds. There must have been hundreds. During the last few days there has been a most noticeable increase in the Dunlin and Ringed Plover population of the estuary.

At noon two Ravens soared in circles high above the sands and occasionally called "Quock! Quock!" While I watched they did not once beat their wings but circled about like Buzzards.

During the whole of the day Swallows have been with us, either above the sands or over the house roof. In the evening they swooped and dived round about the house and almost came in at the doors and windows. They are slowly gathering into large flocks in preparation for the long journey. Starlings also came to the house in hundreds this evening and, at one time, perched on the ridge tiles from one end of the roof to the other, and packed so closely that not another bird could have found perching room. The young of the year are exquisite creatures at the moment for their plumage is in transition from juvenile to that of first winter. Their heads and chests are still brown, but their flanks and bellies are black beautifully spotted with white, and some white-spangled black feathers are beginning to show on scapulars and mantles.

On Cob Lake, this evening, there were ten Ruffs, that is eight live Ruffs and two dead ones, these latter victims, I suspect, of another of those " sportsmen." The Ruffs fed close by the bodies of their companions and, on one occasion, one of them stepped on to a half-submerged corpse.

SWALLOWS ABOUT THE HOUSE

121

SEPTEMBER 2ND. To Porth Cwyfan this evening. The tide was out and the dark weedy rocks were uncovered. Crossing the raised shingle causeway we climbed the stone steps leading up to the grassy platform on which the little church stands and, walking to the seawards side, looked down at the rocks. Parts of the dark weed-covered rocks were alive with feeding Turnstones. How they worked! and with what vigour they threw over piles of seaweed! Among them were several cock birds in their summer plumage of black, white, orange, and chestnut. (They always remind me of a tortoise-shell cat in colour.) Near them, and at rest was a company of Golden Plover, adults and young. Some of the adults still retained the black breasts of summer, but most were in various stages of moult, and among these the young birds of the year were like newly-minted coins among old and tarnished ones. Presently we descended to the beach and were watching Ringed Plover when there was a gentle swish of wings behind us and, looking round cautiously, we saw four Bar-tailed Godwit. For all the fear they showed we might not have been there for they began to feed at once ten yards away from us. Here the beach was of wet sand closely pitted with worm-holes and castings. Stealthily we turned round and approached nearer the feeding birds. They ignored us. And now we saw that they were very tired, so tired that they had not the energy to carry their wings in the normal position—above the tail—but let them droop over their flanks. When a gust of wind came they staggered about and were almost toppled over. But they were determined to feed and so absorbed were they that we approached to within sixteen feet before they lifted their heads. Then to their feeding once more, their bills, at times, buried in the sand up to their heads, or again pecking here and there on the surface and uttering little querulous notes as they found a little energy to chivvy each other. We approached closer, to within twelve feet, but that was the limit they set, and they took wing, circled round us and came back to the same area of worm-riddled sand again. They staggered weakly as they alighted but were at their feeding immediately. All four were birds of the year, and we speculated on how far they had travelled that day for never before had we seen such tired, wing-weary birds. After I had made some notes we left them to their feeding.

WEARY BAR-TAILED GODWITS

122

SHOT RUFF

SEPTEMBER 3RD. Immediately after breakfast I went to the road by Cob Lake for the purpose of making studies of the Ruffs. Two were on the mud between the shore and the road not more than ten yards away. I pulled up and they scarcely troubled to look up from their feeding. Almost at once four others came from across the pool and, alighting by them, commenced to feed with the same concentration. The light was good and the birds so close that I at once began my note-making. Delicately they stepped in the shallows picking here and there at minute spots and rarely plunging their bills under water. Food was taken from the mud, from grass and weed-stalks, and one bird pecked at an empty cartridge case the shot from which may have killed one of its companions a few days ago. There was a noticeable difference in size of individual birds and one, paler of breast than the others, was by far the biggest bird. With them was a Lapwing which looked heavy and big by comparison. At such close quarters all the details of their exquisitely laced wings and scapulars were revealed. The large pale bird had the palest cream lacing, while some of the smaller birds had a rufous tinge about their pale parts, and especially on their necks and breasts. I gazed and memorised all I could of their form and colour until quite suddenly, without sound or warning, Ruffs and Lapwings flew off and away down the pool.

SEPTEMBER 5TH. This morning we awoke to a landscape half hidden by sea-mist and drizzle, the first rain for a month. It was good to see and feel after the heat but the rain cleared while the morning was young, and away in the west a streak of blue could be seen. Soon the hilly tip of Lleyn showed like an island far out beyond the bar, and gradually the clouds rolled from the peaks of the Rivals and their neighbouring heights and, by eleven o'clock, as the tide was beginning to widen the river, the lower slopes of the Snowdon range were uncovered and were grape-blue under the shadowing cloud. By early afternoon the mountains were clear-cut even to Snowdon's peak and their blueness, by contrast, made the far sand-dunes glow warmly. The rippled tide, which now covered the sands gleamed and glittered with a myriad points of light, and over it the gulls floated lazily. I could not work because of it all, but to-day will be remembered not only for its grand effects but chiefly, I think, because of the Swallows that came to the house. They came in hundreds, twittering excitedly all about the roof and the garden, and in the afternoon the slates of the roof as well as the ridge tiles were populated with them as they basked in the bright sunlight. Many were young birds, but there were a few long-tailed, chestnut-throated adults with them. W. and I agreed that we had never seen a more exquisite sight than this. On the warm slates some of them

123

rested on their sides with one wing and tiny foot turned skywards as if revelling in the warmth. Others preened vigorously, and some young birds crouched and asked for food whenever a flying bird approached them, even when that flying bird was a young one like themselves. Many times I saw tiny morsels of food passed from an adult to a young one while they were on the wing. Tirelessly they flew around the chimney-stacks, over the garden, and over the sands where some, for a moment, rested before again joining the excited throng. Abruptly every bird would " panic " from the roof, with a great *brrrr-r-r-r* of wings, for no apparent reason, then they would return with increased twittering. A big hen Kestrel passed over and caused one of these sudden flights and several Swallows separated from the main flock and, speeding upwards, swooped at the Kestrel until she, quite unperturbed, came down and rested on top of a telegraph pole by the road.

SWALLOWS ON THE HOUSE ROOF

Sometimes Starlings added their numbers to those of the Swallows and perched on ridge tiles and chimney stacks in close-packed groups. They, too, were mostly young birds, and gave us almost as much pleasure as did the Swallows. Hordes of Sparrows appeared on the garden walls, and at one time, what with Swallows, Starlings and Sparrows, the air about the house just seethed with birds. And so the day went on, with the mountains growing more and more impressive as the sun moved westward and began to throw great blue shadows from ridges, shoulders and precipices. The Swallows left us in the evening. Over the blue Rivals a long line of birds, like a wispy cloud, wavered and undulated, and as they came nearer in ever-changing formation we saw that they were Lapwings. Above the far dunes they poured down and swung over the sand, eventually to alight where a long line of Curlew rested far down the river.

It was impossible to stay indoors on such an evening so we went along to Cob Lake. In the main area of water ten Dabchick bobbed and dived. Their numbers have gradually

124

DABCHICK

increased since a single bird made its appearance on the lake in July. By winter, if previous years are any indication, there will be a flock of between thirty and forty. Under the earthy bank of the peninsular a Snipe rested and, with it, a smaller wader which was neither a Redshank nor a Dunlin. The light was failing and the bird was in shadow and, peer as I would through the telescope, I was unable to identify it. So it remained a tantalising mystery. On the dark mud by the roadside, and almost under our noses, a Ruff had been resting, and only when it ran to the water's edge did we see it; it was quite solitary. We watched the blaze of red and gold fade in the western sky and, turning to the mountains, we saw that Snowdon had put on his nightcap of cloud.

SEPTEMBER 6TH. After a day of work indoors we went out in the evening and found ourselves eventually gazing over the Menai Straits from the road which skirts the shore at Foel Ferry. The tide was low and the sandbanks of the straits were uncovered as also were the mussel beds and shingle stretch of the near shore. We saw that there were birds on the mussel beds

FOEL FERRY

CAERNARVON CASTLE

but, for the moment, we were distracted by the grandeur of the mountain panorama in front of us. From the quarried sides of Penmaen Mawr in the east to the peaks of Yr Eifl in the west the great hills stood, beautiful in the evening light, their shoulders and precipices dappled by cloud shadow. Snowdon was cloud-capped and in gloom all the time. Across the water, to the south-west, Caernarvon town lay, sometimes in golden sunlight, sometimes in shade, and it was remarkable how frequently the castle alone was sunlit while the rest of the town was shadowed by cloud. But our real objective was birds, and glasses and telescope were at length lowered to a more terrestrial angle where they at once picked up Oystercatchers on the mussel beds, with Curlew and Redshank. I was anxious to see just how the Oystercatcher dealt with mussels, and concentrated on one bird which was most active among the shells. First it would stand alert and watchful then suddenly dash forward and jab downwards with its bill and, at the same time, give a wrenching twist which always dislodged the desired morsel. Not once did I see the bird lift a shell from the ground and I can only conclude that it waited until it saw a mussel shell open and instantly dashed in and prised the occupant out of its shell. But the bird's actions were so rapid that it was difficult to be certain of its exact method of extracting the mussel. There was, however, no difficulty in discovering the method of a Common Gull with these shell-fish. This gull we watched was solitary and lame, for one of its legs was twisted out of position and was stiff and useless. The gull hopped on its sound leg among the mussels, selected one and flew up with it until it was above the concrete causeway which runs down the beach to the jetty. The gull approached the causeway at right angles to its length but did not drop the shell on this flight; instead it banked round and flew either up or down the length of the causeway dropping the mussel which hit the concrete and broke the shell. Rarely did the gull need to drop the shell more than once. This reasoned use of the causeway was in marked contrast to the behaviour of a Herring Gull which also flew up with a mussel held in its bill. Obviously ignorant of the uses of concrete it dropped its shell amid the expanse of mussels below and, on alighting, could not distinguish its own from the thousands which covered the beach but gazed vacantly about it, then gave up its search. Where the shingle becomes a sandy beach four Whimbrel and a Curlew strode about probing here and there with their curved bills. What a big bird the Curlew looked against its smaller cousins!

126

Out in mid-straits, on a great expanse of sandbank, seven white birds rested, heads all facing the same way. Before I could get the telescope on to them they took wing. W. heard them call and at once said they were terns. Their deliberate wing-beats, stronger and less whippy than those of the Common Tern, suggested that they were Sandwich Terns, and a view through the telescope which revealed black crests, white foreheads, and black, pale-tipped bills, confirmed this. It is curious that, in our experience, Sandwich Terns are often to be seen in Anglesey on autumn passage but are less frequently seen during the spring migration. There are reports of them nesting on the island but we have yet to verify them.

SEPTEMBER 7TH. Part of the field pool in Bont Farm ground has, at the moment, an area of hoof-pitted mud exposed between stretches of shallow water, ideal feeding ground for the wader tribe. On past September visits it had given us much in the way of birds and this afternoon it did not disappoint us. About the hoof-holes Dunlin fed or rested, birds in bright

DUNLIN AND CURLEW-SANDPIPERS

young plumage chiefly. Other Dunlin fed in the shallows and it was with these birds that we found the Curlew-sandpipers, about a dozen of them. They were noticeably taller than the Dunlin, trim, snowy-breasted, and with bills more obviously curved than the Dunlins'. They appeared more alert and not so hunched-up as their smaller companions with which they often mixed freely. At rest, with heads sunk in shoulders, they were very like the Dunlin, but always the whiteness of their underparts identified the Curlew-sandpipers. Near the bend of the pool three Ruffs kept company with a small flock of Lapwings and, beyond these, five young Shelduck dibbled away with side-to-side motions of bills. (I have seen no adult Shelduck during the last week.)

We examined the grey hoof-pitted mud carefully for, on a previous occasion, at this time of the year, we had discovered a pair of Temmincks' Stints feeding in this very place. But to-day there were no tiny grey birds creeping from one hoof-hole to another.

We crossed over to the other side of the road to examine Cob Lake. Feeding near the road was a Spotted Redshank, a juvenile beautifully barred and spotted. It stepped about

127

SPOTTED REDSHANK

in the shallows and, when it walked, the leg was lifted high, so high that the leg-joint was raised above the edge of the wing.

When it strode on to the mud its real length of leg was seen. At times, while feeding in the shallows, it moved quickly forward with its bill submerged and also swung it from side to side. When a Heron passed over the Redshank crouched so that its breast was in the water and its neck was drawn in; this crouching position was adopted each time any traffic passed.

Cob Lake is almost cut in two by a grassy peninsula which juts out from the road and, because of this intrusion, it is not possible to see the whole of the Lake from the village end, so we moved along and found, under the far side of the peninsula, a group of nine Black-tailed Godwits intent on their feeding. Long bills were probing deep when my brakes squeaked as I pulled up. Nine long necks were raised and we were regarded for some seconds; then the necks returned to their feeding once more. Once in a while there was a little chivvying and there would be a surprising flash of black and white as wings and tails were opened, but they were hungry and food was their main concern. There were young birds in the flock with dark, brown-laced backs, and several adults in transitional summer-winter plumage.

Enough was as good as a feast. We went home convinced that but for the killers this place would be a paradise for birds.

SEPTEMBER 9TH. A wild day! Anglesey was back to normal with strong wind and racing clouds, and a river whipped into little waves with white foaming tips. Gulls flew low over the sands, and Curlew calls lent added wildness to the day. There were equally wild rumours in the village of the geese having arrived. Someone had seen them sweeping down over Bodorgan to the bar. We shall see!

Workmen are still with us, patching up here and there, and to-day while the joiner was fitting a new wooden sill to the lounge window he managed to drop his false teeth in the cavity between exterior wall and interior panelling. We probed with hooks and wire but the teeth remained tucked away. The joiner took a grave view of the situation, but it was with the greatest difficulty that we kept our faces straight. The joiner's boss had to turn away several times for a silent, shaking burst of mirth. However, work went on, a new sill was fitted and finished and everyone, except John the joiner, thought that the teeth were finally entombed. At five o'clock, when joiners' work was officially over, toothless John went outside with hammer and chisel and began to pound away at the exterior wall. Soon he had

made a hole that went right through to the cavity, and John, coming upon his teeth from the side instead of from the top, recovered them in triumph. He put them carefully in his pocket and wished us " good night."

Later I went to the river for a dip. Except for the birds I had the beach and the river to myself, and very exhilarating it was. Over the wide sands there was the wind streaming past, then the seething, slapping waves in the river, and the Gulls, and Lapwings, and racing grey clouds overhead.

At dusk I was on the road by Cob Lake. Several men with guns hung about, on the Cob and the road, for in this strong wind they expected duck to fly low. Two young Shelduck got up from the lake and someone behind the Cob fired at them, and missed. A wild day with the promise of an even wilder night!

SHELDUCK

SEPTEMBER 10TH. When I went to the lake at noon to-day the wind had abated to a fresh breeze. At the village end of the water was a young Herring Gull, an adult Black-headed Gull, and a Bar-tailed Godwit. I was about to focus the glasses on the Godwit when there was a sharp report from the Cob, the whine of a bullet and a spurt of water near the young Herring Gull. The Black-head jumped but did not fly, the Herring Gull staggered, and the Godwit merely jerked up for an instant. On the Cob was a youth with a ·22 rifle. Again and again he fired, and missed. He then came off the Cob and on to the spit of ground that runs into the lake, from which point he proceeded to fire at the miserable young Herring Gull until he killed it. I, thinking he was intent on murdering the Godwit, got out of the car and put the bird up. The youth gathered his dead gull and when I asked him if it was necessary to kill it he replied, " Oh, yes! Gulls are becoming a menace." He then called the Godwit a Stint, which remark seemed to be a just measure of his bird knowledge. This pale-faced youth was a rifle enthusiast and carried a beautiful weapon with the very latest in sights, and had had the stock adjusted for his peculiar length of arm, yet he expended at least a dozen bullets in his efforts on the gull, having first broken its leg before finally killing it. He told me quite a lot about rifles and I told him something about birds, but I fear the seed fell on stony ground for, during the afternoon I again heard rifle shots.

In the evening the lake and the Cob were undisturbed except by the wind which had risen again and was blowing with some strength. Cream-coloured foam was blown to the edge of the lake and rested in the shallows in long frothy rolls behind which the water was almost calm. Five Little Stints took advantage of this comparative quietness and fed in the lee of the foam. At times the wind whipped off the top of a foamy pile and the Stints were enveloped for a moment in the flying spume. This did not perturb them in the least and they carried on with their feeding. Behind another pile of foam, which had been interrupted in

129

LITTLE STINTS

its landward progress by tufts of grass growing from the mud, were several Curlew-sandpipers. In the high wind they were hunched and necks were sunk into shoulders so that one did not get the impression of elegance which is apparent on calmer days. Their habitat of foam and grass-tufts was exquisite.

At the far end of the lake were five young Shelduck, well grown and sleek, and near them were three Bar-tailed Godwit, pale-buff birds against the dark reflection of the Cob. The Godwit were not feeding but stood hunched against the wind and looked as if they could never become the long-necked, stream-lined birds of their more active moments. The young Shelduck, heedless of the wind, strode about with their bills flat on the mud, swinging them from side to side, absorbed in their feeding. A sudden squall of rain, which the wind drove directly into the car prevented the using of field-glasses and brought my watching to an end.

SEPTEMBER 12TH. Yesterday's weather was so bad that all the people I met this morning began their conversation with " What an awful day was yesterday! " Awful it was, for, from early morning until late at night, a south-west gale swept the island bringing with it torrential rain in such quantities that the gutters and spouts refused to take the roof water, which gushed over and splashed down walls and windows and made great pools on the drive. The gale roared away until late evening, then gradually became less fierce and subsided to a fresh wind.

When I went to Cob Lake at nine o'clock this morning I found that the water-level had risen considerably, and ragwort which was growing on dry land forty-eight hours ago was now awash in several inches of water. At first no birds were to be seen about the wind-whipped lake, then the glasses picked up a flicker of movement, grey against the grey water.

130

I moved farther along the road and found a young Black Tern hovering and dipping near the shore of the peninsula, now flooded so that it had become an island. The telescope was focused on the tern and revealed that it was a bird of the year, strikingly black and white in the head and with dark brown patches on each side of the breast. Back, tail, and wings were a smoky-grey and the scapulars had a brownish tinge about them. Head to wind the tern hovered, then dipped, taking food delicately from the water surface, and working into the wind as it did so. Then, lifting, it allowed itself to be blown to the shore, where it again hovered and dipped moving against the wind. Not once did it plunge for food beneath the surface as is the manner of Common Terns when feeding. After a time it drifted down-wind and came to rest on the grass of the peninsula where, among the tussocks and the ragwort, I could see its pied head moving. It did not rest for long but was up again and, swinging away towards the village, resumed its feeding. I followed and had the pleasure of a close view as it hunted near the road. It was a delight to watch, especially when it began a systematic hunt of the shore vegetation, and dipped to take food from leaves and stems of grass and ragwort, some of which were still in flower. The food on the green plants seemed to its liking for it worked the shore methodically as I followed it. At times the tern was but a few feet away and once I thought it was about to fly in at the car window. Eventually I had to leave the storm-driven sprite and thanked it for being such an accommodating model. Some hours later, as W. had expressed a desire to see the tern, we went to the lake but it was not to be seen either on lake or field pool.

BLACK TERN RESTING

SEPTEMBER 16TH. There are persistent rumours of geese having been seen, both flying up the marsh and resting on the estuary sands. The rumours vary; sometimes the geese are Barnacles, and sometimes White-fronted, but so far I have not had a glimpse of them. This evening, hoping that I might be more fortunate, I went along the road and stopped by the lake. To while away the time I began to make a drawing of the two very substantial gateposts which flank the beginning of the lane to Bont Farm, and of the landscape beyond, with the straight rutted lane running into it. The evening was grey and windy, and behind one of the gateposts two shooters were sheltering, and they, too, were waiting for the geese or anything else which might turn up. With them were two spaniels one of which sat in the lane mid-way between the two posts, gazing intently up the marsh. It was so immovable that I included it in the drawing. I had been working for some time when, happening to look in the direction of the estuary, I saw, approaching, a great host of duck, probably three to four hundred, which had been resting down the estuary and were now coming into the marsh to feed. The Mallard, for such they were, came on in a series of rough V or crescent formations. They were high

BONT FARM GATE

and out of range, but the gunmen did not see them until they had passed over and were speeding on up the marsh with the wind behind them. Muttered remarks, not complimentary to high-flying ducks, came from behind the gatepost. Further along the road there was a sudden bang! and a Curlew drifted across, losing height all the time and obviously wounded. It managed to clear the lake and the Cob and was lost. No one attempted to recover it. Then, but for the wind, all was quiet and no more birds passed over. The grey evening became greyer and darker and I was about to turn for home when three Greenshanks came calling over

GREENSHANKS

the lake, settling on the grassy verge near the road. Again the gunmen were huddled behind the gatepost and did not see the Greenshanks which were now foraging busily in the shallows, and murmuring with quiet notes very different from their usual high call-notes. I was on tenter-hooks lest the shooters should discover them, and was relieved when a passing bus put them to flight. They sped away down the lake and out of the danger zone.

I returned home with a drawing of two massive gateposts but without any goose notes, for no geese were seen that night. Marks of the shooters are much in evidence. The corpse of a young Cormorant lies on the Cob; in the water of Bont field pool a dead Common Gull raises a wing and tail grotesquely from the muddy bed, while an immaculate Black-headed Gull lies dead on the bright green grass of the shore. There is a Heron about with a great gap in the flight feathers of his right wing and on each side of the gap other feathers are twisted back and stick up untidily. Empty cartridge cases are strewn about the Cob and the roadside, for, for some unexplained reason, shooters here are allowed to shoot from the King's highway. On one evening recently a large car was seen to pull up by the lake, shots were fired through the open car window at birds by the shore, a retriever dog jumped out and gathered the corpse or corpses, and the car drove off. Alas for all the rules and regulations!

SEPTEMBER 19TH. Feeling that, of late, I had spent too much time in the studio I escaped, on this bright windy morning, to the sands of the estuary and from the lonely expanse gazed at the surrounding countryside. Gales from the south and west during the last few days had left their mark on the landscape. The salt-laden blasts had turned the hawthorn hedges brown; those nearest the sea looked burnt and dead. Many trees, particularly sycamores, were salt-burned, and some of their leaves, prematurely withered and browned, had dropped from the twigs and gathered in the roadsides and under the hedges. Looking at the wooded hillside of Bodorgan on this morning of bright sunlight, great clouds, and wind, it seemed as if autumn was indeed upon us, for no fresh green was to be seen in all those acres of woodland, only the subdued brown of the deciduous trees and the dark greens of the conifers.

CURLEW DOWN THE ESTUARY

Black Tern

GULLS FEEDING IN THE SURF, LLANDWYN

Those harbingers of autumn, the Knots, were on the shore in a compact flock of perhaps a hundred birds, and a much larger flock of Curlew lined the bank of the curving river. When I approached the Curlew and focussed the glasses on them they lifted from the sands, all piping melodiously—a wonderful chorus and a beautiful sight.

I plodded over the wet sand to the cockle beds, a mile down the estuary, where I found the shore strewn with bundles of seaweed in which were entangled cockle-shells, still paired but all empty. What a feast the gulls and Oystercatchers must have had after the gales! Up to this point the sand had been wet but now, as I approached the bar, I came upon an expanse of cleaner sand which was dry and was blown by the wind in long waving streams towards me. Thinking to avoid this I cut into the dunes which flank the southern side of the estuary and made my way across a flat pan which, in winter, holds great pools. This pan, open to the shore, collects a strange assortment of debris from the tides, and to-day there was everything from a bullock's skull to solidified blobs of black oil-waste. Bones, shells, bottles, glass floats, bits of rope and splintered timber were strewn about this beach-comber's paradise. I traversed the length of the pan then came up against the high dunes and began to climb through them, and once more met blown sand which streamed along the gulleys and poured in plumes from the high crests of the dunes. Deciding that the open shore was a pleasanter place I floundered through the hollows and hummocks and came out on the wide sands which face the sea proper, having cut off the point of the dunes nearest the bar. It was an exhilarating shore this morning. Great white rollers, line after line, hurried in before the west wind, curled and broke in a seething expanse of foam which stretched from the rocky point of Pen y Parc to the jagged rocks below the lighthouse of Llandwyn Island. Not a soul was to be seen on this two-mile stretch, unless the gulls could be deemed souls, for, near the point where the breakers were pounding the first rocks of Llandwyn, there was a great assembly of Herring Gulls. It was a brown gathering, for the greater part of the flock consisted of birds of the year. They were crowded by the water's edge, some in the shallows of the spent wave, others standing in the white foam, and still others floating on the deeper surge. It was clear from their behaviour that the waves were bringing in some desirable food, for at intervals a gull would plunge forward with a sudden opening of wings and capture something

134

from the foam. Just behind the gulls a few Oystercatchers stood and watched the activity but did not attempt to take any part in it.

Presently I reached the low causeway of rock and concrete which connects Llandwyn to Anglesey. Storms had torn great holes in it and, in a few years, if repairs are not made, the turbulent waves of the west shore will surge unrestricted over the narrow neck and into the more sheltered east bay.

Above this quiet eastern shore of the island I sat down and watched six Mallard preening in the company of two Cormorants on the rocks below, an unusual combination. The moment the Mallards saw me they took wing, and their sudden departure alarmed other Mallards which had been resting on the rocks farther along the shore for these, too, hurriedly left the shelter of the rocks and, in small groups, sped across the bay towards the sand-hills.

Fifty yards from the shore two Razorbills floated comfortably, bills and tails pointing upwards, pale throats and chests of their winter plumage conspicuous against the black of their upper parts, and the blue water. While I was watching them a tern flew across my field of view, then another, and another. The first was black of crown, the other two had white foreheads. All three had the long whippy wings of either Arctic or Common Terns. Soon others came and all were flying southwards along the shore, sometimes lingering to plunge to the surface, or to approach nearer to the shore, but always maintaining their southerly course. I could not with certainty identify them for not once did they call, and none rested on the rocks. When the migrant terns had gone I crossed the rugged spine of the island to the ruins of the ancient church. Its three grey walls, and its arched window openings, devoid of mullion and tracery with which they must once have been graced, are exposed to all the winds that blow, for the ruins stand high, and from them the prospect of land and sea is magnificent. East, south and south-west stood the great hills of the mainland—fifty miles of noble contours. From south-west to north-west stretched the wild sea, and then Anglesey filled the horizon, jagged coast to the north-west, rolling farm land to the north and north-east, and a waste of sand-dunes to the north-east and east. As I lingered there a Wren moved

THE RUINS OF LLANDWYN

135

YOUNG HERRING GULLS

among the grey tumble of stones, a brown mouse or a bird, creeping here and there in holes and crannies and undergrowth. I was reluctant to leave this place, but the roar of the waves pounding the rocks of the western shore, and the bursts of spray shooting high above the low headland drew me away, and soon I was feasting my eyes upon the wild scene. From the horizon the great white horses came racing in, their crests now gleaming in the sunlight, now shadowed by cloud, to break themselves on the dark jagged rocks below. Here I came upon more young gulls feeding in the surf but now they were hovering in the wind, above the seething, foaming water below, and plunging to snatch food from the waves. Viewed from above the scene was enchanting, the laced plumage pattern of the hovering birds above the laced foam pattern of the surf. For a long time I sat and watched them and noted that all along the rocks, away to the lighthouse, there were companies of young gulls feeding in a similar manner.

At length I dragged myself away, and skirting the rocks and little bays I eventually came again to the causeway and the wide bay. This time I avoided the wind-blown dunes and walked by the sea's edge. The beach appeared to be devoid of birds, and I had almost reached the bar when I saw two pale spots behind a clump of seaweed. I approached them and found that the spots were Sanderlings in that stage of plumage in which I like them best— juvenile—for then their backs and wings are most beautifully patterned. A sudden stronger gust of wind sent their seaweed shelter rolling up the beach, and pushed before it a wave which threatened to swamp the Sanderlings. Blown and buffeted they ran helter-skelter along the beach pursued by the spumy edge of the wave. Then the sprites began to feed and pecking here and there followed the wave-edge back again as it receded. The wind blew their feathers awry, and sometimes caused them to stagger, but they heeded it not, and ran and fed as the wave dictated.

136

By now the morning had become after-noon, and hunger caused me to turn and face the estuary, and to begin the walk home. Soon I reached the area of blowing sand, but now my back was to the wind, and the sand streamed before me up the estuary in pale waving lines and was not trouble-some.

JUVENILE SANDERLINGS

A mile from home I came upon the Cur-lew flock again which, since the morning, had increased in size, and must now have numbered between five and six hundred birds. As soon as I stood still, and the glasses were levelled at them they all rose as one and filled the estuary with their calls. A short gliding flight and soon they settled again. The Knot, too, were still by the riverside and flickered about in short flights, one moment a conspicuous cloud of pale undersides the next a scarce visible movement of brown-grey against the shore.

ESCAPING EEL

I had almost reached the Cob when a young, pale breasted Cormorant, probably disturbed from the lake, flew over with a wriggling, writhing eel in its bill. For a split second the eel seemed to break free but was grabbed convulsively by the hooked bill before it could fall. Again it thrashed and wriggled and at last succeeded in freeing itself, and dropped to the sands in a place where there was a thin covering of water. The Cormorant followed it down tumbling like an old umbrella, and on reaching the sand stood for some seconds staring at the shiny surface. Then it jumped forward and, with a lightning out-thrust of neck, recaptured its eel and took wing. When it reached the river it planed down and, pushing out its great black webs, skidded along the water and came to rest. It dipped the eel, and after more struggles swallowed it.

I climbed the stony side of the Cob and had nearly reached the road-bridge when I found a dead Turnstone, its body still warm, and with shot wounds in breast and wing.

And so home where I discovered it was mid-afternoon. The smell of a belated lunch was never more welcome.

SEPTEMBER 20TH. There are some days on which nature seems to bestow upon us all she knows of beauty and charm. Rain had fallen in the night and the sun rose upon a sparkling, clean landscape of glittering river and shining sands, clear-cut chequer-board of fields, and wonderful mountain silhouettes under towering clouds. By the bend of the river Redshank, Oystercatcher and Curlew piped to the morning; the sands were full of their calling. It was so calm that the sound of the breakers at the bar could be plainly heard, like a far away continuous thunder.

Work at the drawing-board seemed most inappropriate but it had to be done and gradually the beautiful and alluring out-of-doors was forgotten. . . . But only for a time. At mid-morning three Stonechats arrived and perched on the shore wall and stuttered away cheekily. One of them was a dapper cock bird, very different in appearance from one seen

137

COCK STONECHAT

three weeks ago which was in moult and very delapidated. Now the Stonechats are in good feather and clothed for the winter. I could stay in no longer but walked into the garden where a Robin was tumbling out his cold little song from the top of a privet hedge. This hedge, which faces the morning sun, was haunted by Red Admiral butterflies, and seven or eight of the lovely creatures basked on the warm leaves with wings full open. There were others about the marrows, and one rested—a ravishing spot of black, white and red—on a large pale cream-green fruit. Another rested on the warm sandy soil of the garden with wide-spread wings, body inclined upwards at an angle which caused the hind wings to be pressed on the sand when they resembled some wonderful trailing garment. By the privet hedge is a walled enclosure in which compost is accumulated. A few over-ripe plums had been thrown on top of the heap and these proved irresistible to the Red Admirals for there were at least seven of them all toping away at the plums in ecstasy, or so it seemed, for their wings would slowly open and close as they sipped the juices.

At noon three Ravens flew over the house and, when I focused the glasses on them, it was seen that all three were open-billed as if panting with the heat. Certainly the air was very warm. In the mid-afternoon Swallows came to the house roof again and perched on the gutters just above the kitchen window. Several of them, perhaps members of second broods, retained some of the nestling down on flanks and wings, and these were frequently fed by the parents. Those juveniles which had lost their down were most immaculate, and their sleek shoulders and backs shone in the sunlight. Their dark eyes gazed about them, ever on the lookout for a parent with food and, when they sighted one, they fluttered their wings and opened yellow-margined gapes to take the morsel. Often the parent delivered the food whilst hovering, and was off again the next moment in search for more. I went upstairs to a little dormer window and from there made drawings of the young birds from a distance of five feet. They turned to give me dark-eyed stares but did not move from their perch on the gutter edge, and I was able to make several studies. While I was drawing a cock Greenfinch jumped on to the gutter and scared away one of my models. Then a very spruce pied Wagtail came twinkling along the slates, all wings, legs and tail, halted for a moment, wagged its tail,

of course, and was away. It seems that when the Swallows come to the roof the young Starlings must come also, for they were again on the chimney stacks and the ridge. All the Starlings on the roof this afternoon were young birds. They still retain their brown juvenile head feathers though, for the rest, they are now resplendent in their spangled, first winter dress. I completed my Swallow notes and marked how dowdy and worn was the plumage of the old Swallows. They played about the roof until the evening when, as the shadow of a long, low cloud

THE HOT SUN

in the west crept over the roof, all suddenly left and, winging away over the village, disappeared in the direction of the marsh.

YOUNG SWALLOWS

SEPTEMBER 23RD.   Birds come and go, and nowhere is this constant passage more apparent than by the bend of the river in front of the house.   This morning four Spotted Redshanks were feeding there, or, more correctly, three feeding and one resting on its breast, asleep on a little mid-river rock.   They were with Common Redshanks, and near them was a pale Greenshank, and a Bar-tailed Godwit.   The Greenshank was the aristocrat of the company, slim, quick, and vigorous in its search for food, very upright between the downward strikes of bill, and sometimes almost dancing as it chased some quick-moving prey in the shallows. The Spotted Redshanks were almost as elegant, and they, making use of longer legs and bills, fed in deeper water than their Common cousins.   The Godwit probed away, plunging its bill up to the hilt and beyond, for sometimes its head also was buried.   It seemed a staid and stolid bird against the mercurial Greenshank.   Round the base of a big seaweed-covered boulder a Curlew was hunting.   This bird, usually solitary of her kind, we have come to regard as an old friend, for let other more flighty creatures come and go, she is always hunting by her boulder at low tide, and her prey is always the same—crabs.   Sometimes she captures one which is too big to swallow with ease, then there is a struggle, this often made still more difficult by a harassing gull or two.

At mid-morning a flock of Common Gulls came gliding on rigid wings over the Cob, across the sands to the river where all settled in the water and began to wash.   There were over a hundred birds in the flock and their splashing, dipping, and wing-shaking gave a sparkle and life to that part of the river which seemed to infect the more sedate waders.   Redshanks made short, mad flights about the shore, and the Spotted Redshanks waded belly-deep, nay, wing-deep, among the bathing gulls, and plunged their heads and necks below the ruffled water until, at times, one could see only their backs and tails sticking up.

By twos and threes the gulls walked into the shallows and up the gently sloping sandy bank until there were none left in the water.   Then all preened—a pearly company on the tawny sand. Gradually the other birds, their hunger satisfied for the time, came to the shore or the little rocks and rested, and soon all were still, excepting that big Curlew, which seemed fascinated by its occupation of crabbing.   The three Spotted Redshanks went to a little seaweedy table of rock projecting a few inches above the water and joined the other bird which had slept there during the whole time of my watching.   It must have been very tired for, in a few moments, after the arrival of the three, it tucked its head back and slept again. Its companions preened, then rested on one leg.   The wilder Greenshank vanished from the scene.

JUVENILE TO FIRST
WINTER PLUMAGE

139

CRAB-HUNTING CURLEW

SEPTEMBER 25TH. Early this morning a Heron and a Cormorant, both young birds, provided amusing distraction. The Cormorant was swimming in the river near the house. It swam parallel to the surface with its neck and head submerged, but with its back showing as a black shiny cushion. A young Heron was standing on the edge fishing and as the Cormorant approached it the Heron stared as if in wonderment at this strange thing in the water. Oblivious of the Heron the Cormorant continued its partly submerged progress and, as it passed, the Heron with neck stretched to the full stepped into the water, still gazing with obvious curiosity. With slow careful strides and with intense concentration the lanky grey bird followed the black bulge for some yards before stopping with one foot raised in an attempt, so it seemed, to think this thing out. The Cormorant had now swum some distance away from the Heron which, as if suddenly realising this, sprang to wing and, with three or four flaps made up the distance and alighted in the water just behind the Cormorant's tail. Up came the Cormorant's head and seeing the Heron just behind it let out a surprised " Gwak! " and dived precipitately. The Heron, suddenly realising that its curiosity had taken it near the road bridge, on which

CURIOUS HERON
140

A Greenshank and Spotted Redshanks

men were standing, jumped from the water and, with strong purposeful wing-beats, sped away across the sands to alight at the far bend of the river. The Cormorant resumed its surface fishing, and when it chanced to bring its bill above water I saw that it held a tiny fish; it seemed that the bird had been following and feeding upon a shoal of small fry.

GREENSHANKS FEEDING

SEPTEMBER 26TH. We watch the bend of the river first thing every morning, for some birds are always to be found there, even if they are only the ubiquitous Redshank. They were there in plenty at eight o'clock, running and piping as the rising tide moved them from the little stones in the bed to the sandy edge of the river. But two Greenshanks uttering their own characteristic note, separated from the Redshanks and flew to the opposite side of the river, and there commenced to run along the shore until they were on the stretch opposite the house. There they waded into the water and, laying their bills flat on the surface, they forged ahead, keeping together and almost in step. They did not raise their bills from the water but proceeded parallel to the shore edge, and I think I have never seen anything prettier or more delicate. Soon they reached low seaweedy rocks where they could not continue to run and feed, but among these they pecked and probed, now in full view, now lost in the hollows, but all the time moving towards the road bridge.

Suddenly there was a loud bang, and instantly the Greenshank took flight. One turned downstream and joined the alarmed and flying Redshank, the other raced under the road-bridge and sped away upstream calling all the way.

Later the Redshank returned to the river and a small party flew to a little rock in midstream and crowded on to its weedy, restricted top. Others on the bank began to wade towards the rock, but before they reached it they were afloat, and completed the distance swimming almost in single file. While there was room on the little rock Redshanks scrambled on to it, but soon it could accommodate no more, and those which failed to find standing room had to swim and wade back to the bank. They made a charming picture as they swam with little tails cocked up and necks erect, again almost in single file.

REDSHANK ROCK

141

RIVER BEND AT BODORGAN

SEPTEMBER 27TH. A mile down the estuary the winding river curves abruptly in to the north-western shore, and here, in past ages, it has scooped out a bay round which it curves before continuing its way to the sea. This little bay was our objective this evening, for it was a place of happy memories. Long before we approached it we could see a great concourse of birds above the sands, a noisy crowd of Rooks and Jackdaws evidently enjoying the spacious estuary, for they swirled and swooped about, and almost shouted in their pleasure. Many rested on the sands, a black host with Gulls and Oystercatchers in their midst. As we drew

YOUNG COMMON TERN

142

nearer to them the wary crows took wing and, circling high, gradually drifted towards the great trees of Bodorgan. Every few minutes formations of Curlew passed overhead, all flying up the estuary in the direction of the marsh, while in the middle of the sands there must have been many thousands resting. Their lovely calling was almost continuous.

As we rounded the nearest horn of the bay—a point of low, curiously eroded rocky cliffs—we came upon a most animated scene. Below the homing Rooks and Jackdaws a company of Black-headed Gulls was fishing. With them were eight Common Terns, also fishing. In its progress down the estuary the river glides along smoothly and gently enough, but in the curve of the little bay it suddenly becomes rough and tumultuous and has a decided voice, for here it runs over a rock bed. Above this rough water gulls and terns hovered and into it they sometimes plunged. Often the terns captured a small silvery fish and flew up with it where, if it were not swallowed at once, it invariably attracted the parasitic gulls and a chase ensued. Always gull was out-manœuvred by tern and not once did I see a tern deprived of its catch. Two of the terns were juveniles, white of head and dark of wing-shoulders The others were adult with but the slightest suspicion of the white forehead of their winter plumage showing.

As we intruded farther into the bay gulls and terns swung away upstream and soon the bay was empty. By the shore the gardener's cottage stands high, protected and fortified by a great stone wall with slits in its top through which peep a row of ships' cannon. Somewhere behind the cottage a Green Woodpecker repeated his derisive call. Here the tall trees of Bodorgan Woods come down to the shore. Great Monterey Pines dip their low branches almost to the stones of the estuary, and every year the tides steal a little more soil from their root-hold. On their thick dark branches, rings of old cones still cling, dark and dead, but reluctant to leave the parent branch, perhaps forty to fifty years old.

Our walk continued past the boat-house, and on for perhaps another half-mile to a point where Llandwyn lighthouse showed just beyond the corner of the far dunes, then, the light beginning to fade, we retraced our steps and lingered again in the shade of the dark pines. In the bosky depths a Tawny Owl was rousing and uttering weird husky calls which had none of the high clarity of his mid-winter notes. We tried to imitate the muted call, and each time we were answered from the wood.

In the gathering dusk we made for home, and all the way along the lonely shore we disturbed birds. Lapwings and Redshanks lifted querulously from the riverside, and from the stretches of sand and mud Ringed Plover and Dunlin rose almost invisible in the twilight, their presence betrayed by their calls. We reached our own shore wall as the first lamp was being lit in the nearest cottage.

SEPTEMBER 29TH. We found unusual activity on the beach at Foel Ferry this evening. When we arrived the shore was dotted with stooping figures and half-filled sacks. On the dark weedy beach men and youths bent to their task of filling buckets with shells and, when full, emptying the buckets into the sacks. On the road at the head of the beach stood two lorries.

The mountains were clear-cut and magnificent in the bright evening sunlight, and even Caernarvon, although not remarkable architecturally, except for the castle, looked a most interesting collection of buildings, the golden-yellow light softening the harsh colours and forms, and picking out the bright spots of painted and colour-washed walls here and there. Never had the long panorama of Caernarvonshire appeared more impressive, but the stooping men, if they were conscious of their surroundings, did not show it but bent to their task until

143

MUSSEL-GATHERING BY MENAI STRAITS

all the sacks were full. Wack and I walked down the beach and saw that the sacks were filled with mussels, each sack containing about a hundredweight. These were now heaved on to the backs of the lusty young men who carried them across the mussel-beds, heavy boots crunching shells at every step, up to the waiting lorries on to which the sacks were loaded. Being curious regarding the final destination of so many shell-fish we questioned one of the men on the beach who told us, rather brusquely, that they were to be used as fisherman's bait. However, a second inquiry from another of the men revealed that they were for human consumption, and that they would pass through several stages of cleansing before reaching the customer. He also told us that new mussel beds were being started by deliberately planting young mussels in localities where before they did not breed. We looked about us at the shelly expanse of the beach and could not discern that the removal of two lorry-loads had made any impression on the mussel population.

ANGLESEY THATCHING

After the lorries, with loads of sacks and men, had gone we lingered and watched the shoulders and flanks of the mountains turn a rosy pink. When the shadow of Anglesey had darkened the castle and was creeping slowly over the foothills of Caernarvonshire we came away.

LLANDDEUSANT MILL

SEPTEMBER 30TH. A dreamy quiet morning of soft cloud and blue sky decided the afternoon for us. " We'll do a Cobbett, a Rural Ride, right to the other side of the island, and see what has been happening during this not by any means quiet September." Two o'clock found us crossing the old humpy bridge at Aberfraw, a bridge not made for motor traffic, but which, in my case, happened to be the most convenient way to a petrol pump. Here our eight horses drank their fill, then away we went, heading nor'-nor'-west as consistently as winding narrow lanes would allow.

The countryside was full of colour. Beyond the grey stone walls bordering the road lay great stretches of stubble awaiting the plough, and on these golden fields flocks of geese were foraging. Geese seem to have done well on the island for there are flocks everywhere, and it is to be hoped that a local proverb " Good for feather, bad for wool " has not been fulfilled this year. Certainly there seems to be a goodly number of sheep also. The stackyards were full of hay and corn, and there were some pretty examples of the local thatchers' art which, at its best, is as neat and workmanlike a job as any stack-thatching I know. It has to be efficient for the winds of Anglesey are merciless and search out all slip-shod work. About the stacks and farmyards wandered droves of turkeys, scratching and pecking here and there, enjoying their brief life.

The recent rains have produced a late growth of grass on the pastures and to-day their

145

bright fresh green contrasted with tawny stubbles and the grey, rocky outcrops, these latter being a feature of the interior of the island. It was evident, too, that the recent salty gales had affected the foliage of trees and hedges across the whole extent of the county. Hawthorn hedges were almost stripped of leaves and, in many places, were aglow with crimson haws, so much so, that some of the lanes were flanked with solid banks of crimson. Sycamore and ash had suffered greatly from the salt winds and their leaves were brown and shrivelled and many had fallen to the road.

Past the little white cottages and the grey farmhouses we went; past the little grey churches with their tiny bell towers at the west gable, and the old sail-less towers of windmills (plain evidence of the amount of corn which must have grown in Anglesey's fertile soil years ago), until we came to Llanddeusant where there is a windmill, the only one on the island I believe, which still retains its sails. There it stood, on high ground to the west of the village, its four great arms fixed and immovable, and the slats of the sails hanging loose and derelict, the playing perches of Jackdaws and the look-out posts for Kestrel and Carrion-crow. Daylight showed through the curved timbers of the roof, through which the weather penetrates to the interior timbers, hastening their decay and destruction. I went through the wide door at the base of the great stone tower and the first interesting detail I came upon was an oblong board fastened to the wall, at eye level, on which was set forth the tariff for grinding. Wenith, Haith, Geirch—Wheat, Barley and Oats were listed. To the left was the great chute down which the meal must have streamed and, below it, the wooden bins for receiving the meal.

THE MILL-STONES ON THE FIRST FLOOR

146

ANGLESEY FARMLAND

I climbed the wooden steps to the first floor, and there found three grindstones, big as cart-wheels, their axles geared to a great master cog-wheel whose axle was the thick centre shaft which must have been, in its turn, geared to the sails. Above each mill-stone was a hopper, the top of which was open to the second floor and into which the grain was poured. It left the hopper by way of a spout at the bottom, this being directed to a hole in the centre of the grindstone, the grain passing from hopper to stones between which the grinding took place, the meal passing along grooves in the stone to the chute, and so to the bins on the ground floor.

Though the mill had not worked for many years the dust of the flour still seemed to linger about the interior and it did not require much effort to imagine the great cog-wheels and stones turning once more. But decay has gone too far I fear and the grand old mill slowly follows the fine old craftsmen who made it, into oblivion. We left it wondering sadly if, on our next visit, it would still be inviting the winds with arms akimbo, or whether we should find a limbless stone tower similar to all the other mill-towers in Anglesey.

And now we entered more airy upland country where Rooks and Jackdaws played with Gulls and Kestrels over windswept fields and scanty wind-blown trees, a district where great monoliths stood in the middle of fields; a stone wall country, and one of winding, narrow lanes in which one prays that no other vehicle will be approaching from round the next blind bend. We followed the little finger-posts which pointed to Cemlyn Bay and soon the car was touching the stones of the shingle ridge which curves finely round the bay, and which runs between the sea and a lake. On the landward side of the ridge sea-kale grows in great profusion and this sheltered slope is beloved of birds. Cemlyn is a bird sanctuary and is perhaps at its best in midwinter, for then the lake is populated with thousands of duck. To-day there were perhaps a few hundred and almost all of them were Shovelers. There were a few Teal and one solitary Pochard drake. The Shoveler drakes were all in various untidy stages of moult, very different from the immaculate creatures they will be in midwinter. We watched them as we ate some sandwiches, and also watched a Redshank happily swimming from one grassy islet, near the

147

shore, to another; the second time within a few days we had seen Redshank swim. Do they swim more in September than at other times?

Tea finished, we reluctantly turned the car, and soon we were climbing to the wild uplands behind the bay, by a little road which was new to us. From this high ground it seemed as if the whole of Anglesey lay below us, mile upon mile of rolling country dotted about with grey farms and little white cottages, away to Caernarvonshire and its great blue mountains in the south and east. Slowly we travelled home, the warm light of the setting sun mellowing the grey stone walls and farms, and turning into a veritable blaze the orange-lichened roofs of barn and byre. Westward the sun was sinking between lines of red and purple cloud whose edges were aflame with golden light, and when we reached the sea again near Rhosneiger its waves were a deep purple tipped with rose and gold. The sun went down red behind a purple haze of cloud which lay on the horizon. Land and sea became shadowed, all except the mountains which, as they caught the last of the light, took on the most delicate lilac tint. Slowly the shadows crept up their flanks until only Snowdon's peak was lit, and gradually it, too, lost the rosy light and became a blue silhouette against an almost green sky.

In the deepening twilight we reached home and, before going indoors, gazed down the length of the estuary. We still find it difficult to believe that we really live and work in this place so close to the birds and the sea. However, there they were, the great white drifts of gulls just discernible on the darkening sands, the calling of unseen Curlew, and the distant roar of the breakers at the bar.

Low over the house a formation of belated gulls passed, their white undersides catching the last of the afterglow, and as they disappeared in the dusk we unlocked the door and lit the lamps, feeling well content.

ESTUARY AT SUNSET

148

Drawings in the Text

Drawings in the Text

Index

Index